CH

D1572275

Authenticity in America

A Memoir of Rebellion & Dual Identities

I dedicate this book to all first- and second-generation American women. You are not alone on the journey toward an authentic life.

For more information, please contact:
Mascot Books
620 Herndon Parkway, Suite 320
Herndon, VA 20170
info@mascotbooks.com

Library of Congress Control Number: 2018909259

CPSIA Code: PRFRE1218A
ISBN-13: 978-1-64307-234-0

Printed in Canada

Authenticity
IN AMERICA

A Memoir of Rebellion & Dual Identities

By

Shahira Niggin Qudrat

We all have stories.
What is yours?

Introduction

I know who I am: *a proud Multi-American woman of Afghan descent whose intent is to inspire women to embrace their authentic purpose so that, together, we can increase our influence and transform our world to be more equitable.* My purpose in writing this book is to share my story from the viewpoint of a 1.5 generation American (someone who enters the United States at a young age and finds themselves relating to both first- and second-generation people). Growing up between two cultures can be a chaotic experience. America and Afghanistan couldn't be more different countries in the context of culture, civilization, or history, yet elements of both exist within me and the many others who call themselves Afghan-American.

When I wasn't rebelling against my dual culture identity, I was standing halfway between them, paralyzed by the fear of making a choice that was too American in the eyes of my family and community, or not American enough in the eyes of my friends or colleagues. The saying goes, "you can't make everyone happy," however for the majority of my life I tried to do just that and failed miserably. As you read my words today, know that the constant navigation of existing within two worlds does not end for people of dual-identities. Identifying myself as a *true* American took a lifetime; not just in citizenship, but in mindset. Finding the courage to listen to my heart, trusting my intuition, and doing things my own way wasn't easy or comfortable, but it was the truth. It was a scary truth.

As with most people who seek purpose and meaning to existence, I often questioned what piece I was responsible for in the jigsaw puzzle of the universe. During my pursuit of purpose, I noticed a pattern of personal success when following my intuition, embracing risks, and staying curious about options in the face of disaster. My intentional focus, or staying in this "zone," positioned me to examine my own self from an objective state instead of viewing myself bilaterally as either a "good" or "bad" person. In this frame of mind, taking action and observing outcomes without harsh judgement provided space for internal reflection and alignment. This doesn't mean there weren't consequences when I made a choice—rather, it was a learning experience for the next time I was faced with a similar situation or decision. For someone like me, who always sees the world from two different lenses, finding a zone of internal alignment was an invaluable discovery. I passionately call this space the *Authenticity Zone*, a term coined by me to indicate my elevated state of self-awareness, curiosity, and commitment to learning. My existence in this brain space lessened my cognitive dissonance, and instead of constantly navigating the "right thing to do," I started asking the question, "What if?" This created a paradigm shift that placed the power of choice back into my hands.

Throughout the book, I also use the term the *Comfort Zone*, a popular psychological term describing a state of mind where someone feels safe, secure, and risk-free. The *Comfort Zone* is the opposite of the *Authenticity Zone*. When I was in the *Comfort Zone*, I did not trust my intuition, take any risks, and remained passive about changing negative behaviors and habits. While the *Comfort Zone* was familiar and safe, it often created an environment that stagnated my personal and professional development. As you will read further in the book, staying in the *Comfort Zone* caused me to become inflexible to change and retreat from taking action. Additionally, the combination of negative self-talk and my uncanny ability to find fault in myself and others caused me to quickly dismiss the confidence to transform my circumstances. Staying

> To learn more about the *Authenticity Zone* concept, visit http://resources.AuthenticityInAmerica.com for tools, resources, discussion guides, and more.

Authenticity in America: A Memoir of Rebellion & Dual Identities in the comfort zone appears safer because a person can "coast" through life and take no action; many people do. A breach out of the *Comfort Zone* means diving headfirst into uncertainty and take the risk toward self-discovery. All too often as young adult I was scared to death of rupturing my false identity, therefore I suppressed my inner voice in order to fit in.

The act of living authentically—while not an easy path—is a rewarding one. I make mistakes daily, but remain committed to standing in authenticity because I know how difficult it can be to live in self-deception. The conscious decision to remain curious about opportunities that present themselves, even when we are faced with very difficult challenges, takes daily self-reflection. It's about taking the time to stop and embrace self-awareness as a way of life and accept that vulnerability, while scary, is the only way we can expose ourselves to the truth of who we really are. When one is operating in this state of mind, they are *in the zone*; in harmony with the symphony of life.

We all carry a novel within ourselves. Just like each chapter of this book is unique, so are the various stories that make up your life. As the author of my own life, I choose to share my novel with you. My hope is that my story will demonstrate that no matter how harsh your circumstances might seem, the possibility of a far better future is always ahead. My perspective as an American-Afghan, Muslim woman produces a unique lens that will hopefully open the door for important conversations around feminism, religion, discrimination, harassment, and most importantly, what it means to be an American today.

Let me quickly insert something to dispel any assumptions before we go any further. I am neither a cultural expert nor historian on Afghanistan, nor have I returned to the country since my arrival in the United States. Unfortunately, conflict is still so prevalent in so much of my home country that it makes it difficult to travel there. I also recognize that there are multiple perspectives on any story; however, the historical accounts of my family were recorded by me through the spoken word of my parents and other family members.

Lastly, this book is written in a style that is most befitting to who I am: a conversationalist. Over the years, I have learned that the best way to connect with a person is to strike up a conversation and just listen. Not listening to respond, but listening to learn. This strategy has been an invaluable part of my personal growth, and the people along the way who have shared their stories with me or helped me find my own voice hold a special place in my heart. I want this book to be a conversation between you and me. As humans, we are social creatures who learn from each other, but only when we listen to each other. If we forget this, we diminish the very thing that makes us human.

We are all storytellers, but being an authentic storyteller is risky business. Being authentic means being imperfect and embracing the attributes that make us flawed human beings. Finding your unique path, as I have found and continue to trail-blaze my own, is rough but rewarding. Through hearing my authentic stories, I hope you will be empowered to tell your stories authentically as well. If you are currently in a difficult place, don't think that if you follow my advice, everything will magically become okay overnight. It won't, but you may find similarities between my story and your own, and you may learn something. Of all the things I hope for you, dear reader, my biggest hope in writing this book is for you to know that you are not alone. You picked up this book for a reason, and you are still reading these words. So, let's begin.

1

Authentically American

I hugged her head with my tiny arms. Her thick, black hair prickled my skin as her warm tears collided with my tiny knees. I must have been four or five years old when my mom had an emotional breakdown in my lap. It was a hot summer day in the San Fernando Valley, and we were sitting on our brown vinyl couch watching Bugs Bunny cartoons. As the sound of a firetruck passing our rundown apartment building filled the room, my eyes adjusted to the walls opposite the windows. A siren usually meant we would have a brief disco show in our living room, but this time the lightshow was ignored. All I could think about was how to comfort this woman I had never seen cry before.

Mom usually presented herself like a tall tree, her roots firmly planted in the ground and her head held high when she walked. Her small frame of five feet, two inches was misleading. She was (and still is) a powerful force of nature. However, on that day, my mom was hunched over on the floor with her head in my lap, her hopelessness moving me to share in her tears.

"Oh, honey. Why are you crying?" Mom asked.

"Because you are crying, Mommy. Why are you crying?"

She wiped my tears and hugged me tight. "Mommy is crying because she misses her family in Afghanistan, but you shouldn't be crying."

I didn't know much about Mom's family, but I did know that she was referring to Bebejon and Bobajan *(grandma* and *grandpa* in the Dari language), the elderly couple in a framed picture on a nearby coffee table.

That moment is now a distant memory of the past, but it reminds me that there are many first- and second-generation American women constantly struggling to navigate and make sense of their past and present identities. Mom was far away from her family and experiencing loneliness in a foreign country. She probably wished that her own mother could be with her in that moment, but instead, she found comfort in a young girl who was also developing her Afghan-American identity.

A Clash of Paths

People are quick to forget history. Unless you are Indigenous American you are either an immigrant, come from an immigrant family, or your ancestors were forced out of their homes in shackles and chains to come the United States of America. Though each group had their own share of struggles and triumphs, their stories and experiences continue to shape our present day American culture. It is only because of our ancestors efforts to survive and thrive that we all ended up on this massive piece of land. As first- and second-generation Americans, and the most recent group of people to call the USA home, it is our duty to remind others about the foundations on which this country was built.

I am of two worlds: the United States of America and Afghanistan. Naturally internal discord is created when two extremely polarizing perspectives exist within one human being. Many times the American side of me reacts in frustration and anger at the traditional customs of Afghan natives, and other times my Afghan side reacts negatively to the culture and beliefs of Americans. In reality, the definition of what it means to be American is as complex as a strand of DNA. Be that as it may, if we allow our "Multi-American" values to be driven by assumptions and group think around what is means to be American, we fail to recognize the full story of how this country was built. The "melting pot" metaphor of the American identity loses its appeal when the conformity of a single American identity suffocates the celebration of individuality.

From a strictly biological standpoint the human brain is designed to protect a person from physical and mental harm. In doing so, people can make themselves believe that their personal perspective is the only valid one. Unfortunately, when that happens, consciously or unconsciously, we exclude all other narratives that do not match our own. Layer in varying value systems, mindsets, and the intersectionality of ethnicity, race, religion, or gender identity, and we come face to face with the complex philosophical conundrum we define as the *human identity*. While this book isn't a philosophical discussion about what it means to be a human, it does challenge the meaning of what it means to be an American, interwoven, through and through, within the fabric of the American identity.

While no one person should not have the ability to define another person's level of Americanness, the proposition of living a "Multi-American" life can appear threatening to the single American identity because it suggests a narrative outside of groupthink, and dominant Caucasian narrative. In my own experience, calling myself an "Afghan-American" or "Muslim-American" has not always been easy, especially between the years of 2001 through

2010. However, suppressing my identity as an Afghan-American only caused confusion, not only within myself, but for others who were also finding their place as "hyphenated" Americans.

My definition of living in the *Authenticity Zone* as an American means a person feels a sense of belonging to this country and lives in alignment with the dimensions (ethnicity, race, gender, age, etc.) that make them authentic. When "Multi-Americans" accept themselves as *true* Americans whose roots and heritage are a huge asset to this country, not only will more people be secure in their American identity, but the benefits will envelope our communities and allow them to heal from historical and present oppression. Living in this zone is validation that one is American because one feels secure. Where a person feels secure, they are able to fully participate as a self-aware American whose unique contributions benefit the greater American community. When this happens, I say it's a *bit of magic* because life takes on form that is full of purpose, adventure, fulfillment, and inner peace. Imagine a country where most of its people function this way. Yes—it's possible!

My path to the *Authenticity Zone* was rugged, tearful, scary, joyful, and involved a couple near-death experiences and *a lot* of lessons—none of which I would take back. I still think about Mom and I embracing one another in our small apartment in California. The years following that moment have shown me that no matter the severity of the storm, an unexpected path will appear after the storm passes. The road will have some debris, broken trails, and detours, but a true description for a journey of self-discovery should be as such.

Tornadoes

"Life isn't about waiting for the storm to pass...It's about learning to dance in the rain."
~*Vivian Greene*

Call me crazy, but I am fascinated by tornadoes. Growing up, our family watched a lot of movies with natural disasters. The most memorable movie was *Twister* starring Helen Hunt. It had all the crazy drama you could ask for in a natural disaster movie. The tornado was personified as an evil, family-destroying villain with Helen Hunt as the traumatized child chasing the tornado in search of revenge and closure. Even as an adult, my dreams are filled with twisters forming in the sky as they touch down beside me and my loved ones. In every dream, we are scrambling to find the basement or bathtub of the closest building because that is what we were told to do if we ever found ourselves face to face with such a force of nature. The panic and adrenaline rushes through my body as I hold on for dear life while the windows blown out all around me, and all that is visible is debris and an angry dark sky above. Just hearing the word *tornado* evokes vivid visions of heavy wind and destruction, and the hairs on the back of my neck stand up.

In reality, I have never seen a tornado and just for the record, I have no desire to become a storm-chasing adventurer either. What I do know about storm systems like tornadoes and hurricanes though, is that the most interesting part is the eye. It's a fascinating phenomenon, but the calmest part of the storm is the center. In all the craziness and destruction around the storm, the central operation is often serene and peaceful. Even scientists don't completely understand the "why" behind this.

Playing with Tornadoes

In the storm of our busy lives, each day can definitely feel like a balancing act gone wrong. On any given day for me, the storm can look like a household of seven rushing to get ready in the morning, telling the kids to shut up as they fight over the front seat in the car, attending a business meeting by phone call while driving in to work, getting into work late, and remembering my laptop is sitting on the kitchen table, where I had been working late the night before. As if that weren't enough, the vicious cycle seems to repeat itself when I leave for work the next day. The flow of thoughts that circulate in my head typically sound something like the following:

A full-time career, a family to take care of, children to raise to be compassionate human beings, a house to run, and bills to pay on time—not to mention the business dream that hubby and I are working on in our 'free time' on the weekends. Oh yeah, what are we doing for dinner tonight? Am I going to get my treadmill run in before 10 p.m.? No honey, you cannot go to your friend's house this weekend because we have plans. You need help with your math homework? Shit! I don't remember how to do that kind of math. Yes, I will fill your bottle with milk, darling. Just let me finish washing this last dish!

Are you exhausted by reading that? I am.

The demands in most working women's lives are similar to my own. It seems that the ability to juggle and multi-task are necessary requirements in order to accomplish daily goals. However, at the end of the day, the juggling act leaves many women exhausted and unable to focus on themselves. Before we know it, time has passed us by, and we feel unfulfilled. Women are often told that balance and moderation are key. Agreeing with this idea is simple, but building an appropriate support system around yourself requires thoughtfulness and work, especially for the women who desire to travel the path of authenticity.

When I share with others about my desire to write a book or start a business, the response I usually get is, "Maybe you should wait until things calm down for you," or "How can you afford it?" When those comments arise, immediately the visions of the tornado collide with my life, and self-doubt sets into my brain. The insecure version of myself makes an appearance just to rub it in and say, "See, I told you so! You shouldn't be doing this. Why are you playing with tornadoes? You know they always end in destruction."

Most recently, in writing this book, I placed myself in the midst of a "fear storm." At times it has been downright painful to dredge some of my hardest life experiences to the surface. *What will people think? What judgements will be made about me?* I would often wonder. It is a constant battle to navigate and overcome my insecurities. At the root what makes us most vulnerable as humans, we want to be loved and accepted for who we are. There are elements of my story that would be deemed controversial to some, and there are customs and traditions that will seem foreign to others, but the point of all of this is for you to know that you are not alone and that it is possible to find your own authenticity, even when you feel yourself being pulled to the point of breaking between two countries.

Dancing in the Storm

Let's get real. My inner creative child is afraid—always afraid—of rejection and hurt. Sometimes in my passionate pursuit of explaining to my friends and family about my visions of what our world can look like when there is equity and women are engaging in their life purpose, my hands start flailing all over the place, there are grand bodily gestures, and my speaking voice becomes louder than anyone who is present in the same room. The joint usually quiets down, until it's only me, and the echo of my own voice. While I feel that I am not always articulate (because how can you put the vision in your brain to words?), heads are usually nodding in agreement and there is validation that I am speaking a language that resonates with other women.

There is hope! Whenever the tornado is about to take over my life, I visualize a much younger version of myself, the who was often consumed with adventure and play. I look her in the eye and say, "I need to do this for you girl! You and I know very well that the storm will not pass anytime soon. What is the alternative? To sit by comfortably and keep the boat from rocking?" While talking to oneself may seem crazy to some, validating and facing our fears is a necessary exercise for those who desire taking the authentic path. Yes, my life is busy, but advocating for equity is necessary for me, and hopefully it will serve the thousands of other women out there working to manage the delicate balance of work, life, and the journey of the heart. My own heart and soul are screaming for something more, and the creative child inside of me is looking to build a masterpiece, all while the storm is raging on.

Women want more for themselves: a clear purpose, economic stability, a strong support system, and a way to rejuvenate their fighting spirits. However, success cannot come without time to reflect on what it means to imagine a better life for ourselves, families, or the global community at large. More importantly, our support systems must help create a space that allows us to cultivate an authentic life force. If surrounded by all the right people in one's life, support comes when you ask directly for what you need and want. Once the vision is clear, and the support system is in place, women can take action and put those dreams into motion.

Take a look at the storms around you and *know* that there is calm. Imagine yourself with the eye of the storm planted within your heart as you stand firm in the midst of the crazy wind and rain. Demand space to reflect on your life and explore your passions and desires. All types of work are necessary for the future of this world, and passionate people are often the best in fulfilling their purpose.

Let nature teach you about your ability to find peace within. Re-energize your mind and body, collaborate with those closest to you, and find serenity and support through each other. Women are what make the world go 'round, and men have the ability to become allies. When we learn to love our authentic selves, we can give abundantly to others, and incidentally raise the status quo of gender equity. There is no time like the present to unleash our fighting spirit and spread love where the world needs it most. All people are capable of changing their narrative regardless of gender, social status, or background.

You are the storyteller! Why not tell a story that you love?

Afghan Diaspora in the U.S. in the 1980s

What would you do if you were asked to leave your home-town because an imminent war threatened your family's safety? How would you feel if you could no longer continue your profession because that would require you to start all over with learning basic language skills like a preschooler? How can you begin to teach your children important values when 99 percent of the people around you completely disagree with your beliefs? All of these situations describe what my parents faced when they left Afghanistan to come to the United States.

While modern human migration rates are wreaking havoc on global political geography, it also creates an opportunity for individual human skills and talents come to the surface. Unfamiliar people and uncommon paths present themselves (literally and figuratively) and whether natives or foreigners, people can choose to respond with curiosity, or fear. If you really want to test the idea of human resiliency, you should study the life of refugees. The reality of leaving the only home you have ever known is not glamorous or effortless. The act of resettling in a new country usually means starting over completely, especially if the language is different.

While leaving Afghanistan brought some sense of relief to Afghan refugees during the 1980s, the transition also caused them to feel guilty for leaving a country that desperately needed their skills and talents to re-establish peace and stability. In various conversations with Afghan-Americans who migrated many years ago, I often sensed a bit of "survivor's remorse" when each described his or her state of life in America. "Our poor people have been through the worst: war, starvation, and a corrupt government," they would say as their eyes would grow distant from our conversation in that moment. No one wants to feel their comfort was at the expense of someone else's suffering, yet if those people stayed, they would probably be facing similar situations of loss and hardship.

If the sum of our experiences makes us who we are, what part do our ancestral roots have in shaping us? Moreover, how do people remain culturally authentic when they are not surrounded by these ancestral roots? External factors—such as forced migration due to war and politics—cannot be controlled by the impacted. So, what happens when people must leave their homes, or when families must act or lose their lives? The answers are not straight forward, and the definition of success is not always material. In the case of Afghan refugees, it was simply keeping themselves and their families alive.

The Landscape of the Journey

Afghanistan, a relatively small country with an extensive and proud history, lies in the heart of Asia. It is landlocked and unique in that it is bordered by six other countries, all of which have heavily influenced the subculture of the extremely diverse ethnic groups in Afghanistan today. The capital of Afghanistan is Kabul, which is situated in a valley surrounded by the Hindu Kush mountains.

Hindu Kush literally means "Hindu killer," and my dad used to joke that the mountain range stopped India from overtaking the land, thus giving it its infamous name. While it is a very barbaric translation, my sense is that Afghan people are proud of their independence. Kabul was considered a modern city in my parents' time, and most of its residents spoke the Dari language.

Most people in the more established cities followed a combination of Islamic law, state legislation, and tribal or local customary law. Islamic law, also called Sharia Law, created a set of civil codes that would integrate itself into all aspects of a person's life. Subsequently, application of the laws were based on the chosen interpretation of the leaders, or *mullahs* (Dari for clergymen). The literal and hostile interpretation of Islam has played a perilous role in shaping Afghanistan's past and current history. The war that befell the country in the late '70s was just one of many in a string of violent and corrupt historical accounts.

The culture and laws dictated how one should live as an individual within the social norms. From childhood to the grave, only two things really mattered and set the course for your destiny: your gender and your socioeconomic status. Everything else was details. Gender roles in traditional Afghan culture were exactly how you would imagine within a patriarchal society. Most women stayed home to take care of their children and families, and men were encouraged to provide for their families through work and labor. Parenting consisted of control and discipline. When children disobeyed their parents, they were usually met with verbal or physical discipline. This was the norm, and everyone accepted their role within the family dynamic. Participating in family life required learning responsibility at a young age and contributing to your family in one way or another.

While mothers were teachers in the home, fathers were the family leaders and made the final decisions. For the most part, people followed whatever they were taught at home. On a basic level, there were two paths one could follow: the road of "good" behaviors and religious customs that made you honorable and worthy of heaven; or the "bad" road that led to shame, dishonor, and eventually the fires of hell. In the family dynamic, you were a good child if you obeyed all the rules. If you didn't, the belt and loud shrieks of your parents probably taught you otherwise.

Our own parents told us what to eat, how to dress, and how to be Afghan, according to the way they were raised. I will let you pause here for a moment to imagine what kind of peril that created for the Afghan-American family dynamic.

Disconcerting Values

One example of a deep-seated Afghan value is to respect your elders. This was a blanket statement ingrained in us as children and it applied to all people older than us, regardless of who the elder was. In its purest form, this principle suggests that life is a circle, therefore adults with wisdom and experience should garner the respect of the younger generation. For this reason, nursing homes did not exist in Afghanistan. From the cradle to the grave, families took care of one another and people played their roles to fit into society's expectations. Life comprised of your role in the family dynamic, and if you are a child, the rule was that you should respect your elders.

As children, we often faced conflict between our American view and the Afghan values we all appeared to subscribe to. We silently observed other parents "discipline" (quite harshly) their children, and those difficult moments felt like a lifetime. In my opinion, the punishment never fit the crime. I would run to my mom whenever we witnessed another child be physically disciplined, and she would just hold me. Our tears would silently mingle together in my mother's lap, as we knew we were powerless to do anything in that moment.

Whenever we had the courage to ask our parents why others were punishing their children, we were given angry eyes which said, "Do not get involved! You are a child." Our parents would then sternly reiterate the importance of following family culture and values and remind us that we do not question our elders or get involved in these situations. No one ever explained *why* this was allowed. All that we knew was that we were required to respect our elders, even if they were engaging in less than desirable actions.

Respecting elders without question worked in Afghanistan during our parents' time, because children responded to physical discipline and it was culturally acceptable. Children listened to their parents without question, and they wouldn't push back after receiving a few harsh words or beatings. Besides, it wasn't labeled child abuse in Afghanistan. Physical discipline was considered necessary to teach and enforce the principle of respect and the civil laws conformed to this norm. The problem with us and other children who were living in between the first and second generation of Afghan-Americans, was that we weren't living in Afghanistan or even modern Kabul. We were in a very liberal American environment during the 80s, and we did not see life the same way our parents did.

Americans saw life differently because they were not trying to "protect" traditions that were at risk. America had just come out of the '70s with a new identity which consisted of capitalism and innovative thinking; both aspects which were becoming more gender and racially neutral. White American men and women, although still fulfilling their traditional gender roles, were able to experience more freedom uncovering a collective American identity. Women were free to work, and people were starting to move away from the traditional nuclear family structure that was evident in the iconic 1950s vintage art of Norman Rockwell. As Afghan children and young adults, we so badly wanted to live a "White American" life because to us, "those people" appeared happy and problem-free. Established American families had beautiful homes, fancy cars, fashionable clothes, and none of the heavy emotional baggage that we carried with us everywhere we went.

Recently immigrated Afghan parents who refused to adapt to American norms enforced very strict Afghan traditions in their homes. In some cases, the children accepted their fate and followed the same path as their parents. In other cases, parents were met with many forms of rebellion from the children, especially as they grew into teenagers.

The best-case scenario was parents who were open to change and the integration of cultures. They would talk to their kids about the clashing cultural views, allow themselves to grieve over the traditions that were now being thrown out, and accept that life was changing for them and their children. The parents that were afraid of changing the value systems and traditions—that by definition made them Afghan—took it out on their kids in various ways. Physical, verbal, and emotional abuse became the normal way to interact, driving a wedge between parents and their children. In response, children lashed out and grew further and further away from the things that made them Afghan.

Fearing Change

Many people who came to the U.S. from Afghanistan during the 1980s carried inside themselves a distinct fear. While they no longer feared death or starvation from war, they were faced with a very different type of fear. It was the fear of change that consumed their minds and gave them nightmares. I saw it in the faces of my parents and other close relatives. People were afraid of losing their children to the American culture that surrounded them. Fear drove a lot of families and children to live in bipolar environments; it was "Little Kabul" inside the four walls of their homes, but outside they lived the free and liberal American lifestyle. What was acceptable in one environment was considered unacceptable in the other. For children, change meant going against tradition and making their parents unhappy, so they kept their worlds separate to meet the social demands of both environments.

A "code red" identity crisis appeared amongst the children of Afghan immigrants as psychological issues manifested into conflict and mental health problems. Truthful expression clashed with the need to belong, and people could no longer live as their authentic selves. The traditional way of life did not fit the external environment, and it became difficult to connect to ancestral roots because people didn't really buy into the vision of their parents. If your parents didn't teach you the history or help you understand the "why" behind each custom, it was even harder to accept.

As socially adaptable creatures, we learn different coping mechanisms in order to come to terms with challenging situations. By developing multiple personas, identities, and flexible values, Afghan-American children found ways to fit into multiple social environments. If you could just pretend that you understood and accepted your parents' customs as a way of life, you would not have to deal with constant arguments, and the Afghan community would happily accept you. In my experience, as you will read, this does not work. This description demonstrates what it means to live in the *Comfort Zone*. In the *Comfort Zone*, you do not rock the boat. You are only an observer—a follower.

4

Learning About and Appreciating Family History

My parents were born and married in Afghanistan, as were their parents and their grandparents. As far back as history can outline, Afghanistan's location has made it a prime candidate for war, but during the setting of this story—between the 1960s and late 1970s—Afghanistan wasn't so bad. It was actually one of the more peaceful times in the country's history.

Mommy Dearest

Nooria, my mother, became a caretaker of many at a young age. With her head always in the clouds, books were her preferred method of escape from the reality of her never-ending responsibilities. She often got in trouble for choosing reading over helping her mom prepare a meal for the family.

When I was younger, she shared with me that the French author, Victor Hugo, changed her view on life. After reading *Les Misérables*, my mom felt the moral obligation to live a life that would be meaningful. In her quest to serve others, she developed a soft spot for those less fortunate and vowed to help them reach their full potential.

Although she was not a poet historian, my mother knew much about the literature of her times. She often commented to us that Romeo and Juliet had nothing on Sheereen and Farhad, Afghanistan's version of true lovers. In her eyes, Rumi poems were about love for God, not the interpretation of "human love" that is prevalent in his translated works today.

My mother loved Afghan women poets like Aisha Durrani, and she read the work of other modern romantic poets in her native language. When I was young, she would carry around a large hardcover book that was written by an Afghan woman named Bahar. Bahar wrote passionate poetry for her husband. Of course, no one wants to associate the word "passionate" with their parents, but my mom's love for the written word is a big part of who she is.

My mom was the oldest of six children, which meant that aside from attending school, she was also responsible for cooking and cleaning for her family. While my grandmother was never formally diagnosed, she would suffer from a condition called hyperemesis gravidarum whenever she became pregnant. This condition made it so that she couldn't keep her food down, so she would become weak and end up on bed rest eight out of the nine months of her pregnancies. Since this would render her useless as a dutiful wife and attentive mother, my mother would have to step in as a sort of surrogate mother to her siblings, taking over all the household responsibilities.

My grandfather's parents lived in the same house. *Ma Gul dearest*, his mother, would help my mom through her toughest times by being her soundboard—giving advice, or simply making her laugh. My mother shared that while *Ma Gul dearest* was not the sharpest person, she was very protective of my mother and her siblings. She had a fierce love for her grandchildren and, like my late grandfather, she often spoke her mind without a filter.

Ma Gul dearest wasn't very fond of her husband, my great-grandfather, *Abdul Shukur Khan*, and this often showed up in their day-to-day interactions. Unlike marital discourse that results in divorce in the current day and age, in the traditional Afghan way, if a woman was unhappy, she would make the life of her husband less than desirable. Whenever conflict brewed, she could withhold cooking, cleaning, and sexual pleasure from her husband. The best part was that everyone who lived in your communal home became a spectator to how these scenarios would play out. There was no need for TV because the drama of life itself was the ultimate entertainment.

My mother was the outdoorsy type with a very playful personality. My aunts and uncles still talk about when she would go snake hunting in the fields near their home in Afghanistan. When she found a snake, she would grab it by its tail and swing it over her head. While that wasn't the most humane act toward an animal, I don't know anyone else (except for the late crocodile hunter Steve Irwin) that would have the courage to play with snakes like she did. My mom says the snakes weren't poisonous, but she says that with uncertainty. She was also known for tying strings to the tails of dragonflies. Once she tied the strings on their tails, she would let them fly in the air like kites, curious to see how high or how far they would go. My mother, the snake hunter and dragonfly tamer!

Although my mother wanted to be a doctor, she was not able to score high enough on her college entrance exams to be considered for medical school. So, she became a teacher and taught math to high school kids instead. Although I personally can't think of a worse career, my mother enjoyed her job. She made good money and became a positive role model for her siblings. She was even able to support her parents financially, even though they insisted she not spend her money on them.

My mother thrived in college because she was free to explore her life interests and foster friendships. She went to the movies, wore miniskirts at the height of fashion in Kabul, and confidently walked around in beautiful dresses that accentuated a tiny waistline that other women would kill for. Funny thing is, my mom is much more conservative now and will never admit she was a gorgeous miniskirt-wearing specimen in her early twenties. Luckily, I have the pictures to prove it.

Although it wasn't her first choice of profession, my mother took teaching very seriously. She was loved by her students because she connected with them, and as a result, they produced the best work for her. Her persistence and good humor helped ease the pain of mathematical subjects, and she was adored for it. My mother was having the time of her life and demonstrating her true authenticity as a talented teacher. I can understand why Dad was madly in love with her.

Daddy's Wings

His nickname was *Shayer Agha*, translated in Dari to mean "Lion Man," and he was no less blessed with the soul of one. My dad, Fazal Malek, was the youngest in his family and was very close to his mom, who everyone called *Kokojon*. The first 10 years of his life were spent in the city of Herat, located close to the border of Iran. My uncle often talks about how my dad was the spoiled baby of the family. Everyone showered him with love and gifts.

Being the youngest male in a traditional Afghan family means you do a lot of the errands for everyone else in the household. When my dad was seven or eight years old, he would run to the market and bring fresh meat or bread home for dinner. He was responsible for the family in many ways and was often sent out by his parents or siblings to bring various necessities home.

For the most part, my dad was always running around or spending time outside. He loved the sport of boxing and would spar with his friends and imitate the great Muhammad Ali. My dad even built his own makeshift gym in their yard. He often spoke about how his handmade pull-up bar made him a stronger and taller person. If there was a creative way to challenge himself physically or build a contraption to keep him moving, he did it. His physical fitness and appearance was an important part of his identity.

Though he loved being around all kinds of pets and animals, he was most fond of his birds. He spoke often about the parrots he had trained to greet people when they came in the door, as well as his canaries that whistled traditional Afghan tunes. However, his favorite birds were his magical pigeons. Their captivating performances and fancy tricks were so awe-inspiring that they fueled his dreams when they danced in the sky. Acting as a composer of sorts, my dad would find a long stick and wave it across the sky, whistling instructions to the birds like a song. In unison, the pigeons would dance or move in whatever direction he pointed. He became so skilled with his hand movements that the stick in his hand was almost like an extension of the pigeon wings in the sky. If there was ever a bird whisperer, my dad was one. It was as if his soul was attached to the wings of his pigeons, when he watched his flock flying toward the heavens.

Even though it was popular, *Kaftar Bozee* or "pigeon playing" was considered less than desirable as a sport or pastime in Afghanistan, due to the reputation of businessmen and gambling addicts who had found a way to make a profit from it. Adding to the negative reputation was the belief that pigeon flying patterns were tied to one's destiny, as the patterns represented a form of fortune-telling. It was contrary to the strict religious belief most people held, and further created a bad reputation for those who would partake in the hobby.

Unfortunately, this caused the beauty and skill of the sport to diminish in the eyes of those who were more religious or intellectual, like *Kokojan*. Against her wishes, my dad would find a way to bring some baby pigeons home every year, and every year, *Kokojan* would find a way to get rid of them. After all, she did not want to risk her reputation as a religious woman. My dad hated losing the pigeons that he had worked so hard to train, but over time, he adjusted to the loss. When the pain of losing his flock left him, he would find some friends to give him more baby birds to help create a new flock, one that would make him feel like a magician at least for a little while, before the cycle of loss repeated itself.

Childhood Wounds

As children, we are shaped by our experiences, and my dad was strongly impacted by the breakup of his parents. While people rarely divorced in Afghanistan, couples did separate to resolve problems. In this ironic scenario, the marriage agreement would stay in place, and both families would retain "honor" for staying "together."

When my dad was about 15 years old, his father left his family. My grandfather moved to another state, causing a lot of anger and resentment toward him from all of his children. To make matters more complicated, my grandfather married a second wife a couple of years later. This was acceptable, as many older men had multiple wives and polygamy was prevalent. The pain of my grandfather's departure and betrayal hurt the whole family, but it especially hurt my dad since he was young and still developing emotionally.

Because it was not befitting of her identity within the Afghan culture, *Kokojan* remained married, however she lived with anger and resentment toward my grandfather. She was confident and opinionated in nature and my grandfather was a military-trained individual so needless to say, their personalities were always in conflict. As individuals, they were probably more alike than different, but they were incompatible as a married couple. After my grandfather's second marriage, my dad and his siblings rarely saw their father, but mostly because he was not welcome in their mother's home. The pain was deep, searing, and debilitating; however, *Kokojan* was a strong woman and kept her children close. My dad and his siblings were loyal to her.

Dad was known for being the most caring sibling in his family. Being the youngest of four brothers and a sister meant that he had many nieces and nephews who he deeply loved and cared for. My mother recalls a story that my oldest cousin told her about my dad. A year before my parent's engagement, my oldest uncle and his wife had to flee Kabul quickly because they were targets of political persecution. My uncle's political views were quite different from the traditional views of the time, and it was making a lot of people cross with him. In his haste, my uncle ran away and left everything behind, including his children who were attending school that day.

When my dad found out, he traveled from Herat to Kabul to collect the children from school. While traveling back by bus to Herat, he and the children got caught in the middle of an altercation between Afghan and Russian soldiers. Shooting broke out between the soldiers, and all the civilians were trapped in the crossfire. Although bullets were whizzing by his ears and people screamed in madness, my dad's instincts kicked in. He knew it was up to him to save his family. In the most unselfish way, he threw himself on top of his nieces and nephews, creating a human shield and exposing his heart of gold. Thank God he didn't get hit that day; however, other passengers on the bus were not as lucky. Many were killed by stray bullets.

Back at home, with my grandfather gone and the older siblings busy with their own affairs, my dad was left to his own devices. Post-traumatic stress disorder was not a popular diagnosis when my dad was young; however, the separation of his parents and exposure to extreme violence had taken a toll on his emotional health. He started to cut classes and stray away from home. In his late teens he often ventured out on his own and even traveled across the border to Iran for work.

Being a natural leader, Dad worked in construction project management, street vending, and other entrepreneurial trades. By his early twenties, he had embraced his freedom and become extremely independent. He became an adventurer and enjoyed his youthful years until *Kokojan* decided it was time for him to settle down and marry.

My maternal and paternal grandfathers were first cousins. In the Afghan culture, flesh and blood create deep connections that firmly root in the hearts and minds of families. According to this tribal-like mentality, most people keep marriage relations within the family when possible. Similar to historical accounts of many royal families that kept their legacy alive by marrying within the same blood line, so too were the visions of my grandfathers.

Unlike today's information age, where people can access the social profile of anyone in order to collect information about compatibility, families in Afghanistan relied on the suggestions and recommendations of elders who rated the chances of marital success based on the outward expression or history of a person. Marital unions were initiated when the male's side of the family expressed interest in the chosen female. Once the word was out, the elders of each family would consult to determine if there was a match. Who better to help find your soulmate than the people who knew you best: your parents.

My father's back and forth lifestyle between Iran and Afghanistan caused some worry on the part of *Kokojan*. She no longer had direct control over him and lost visibility into his days. In hopes that my dad would settle down and stay closer to home, she approached my mom's family to ask for her hand in marriage. Surprisingly, my mom's father said no. Given the fact that my dad was still in high school and traveling all the time, the proposal wasn't lucrative enough for my grandfather's oldest daughter. My mom had just started college, and my grandfather made it clear that my dad was not up to his standards. He told *Kokojan* that his family would only accept the marriage proposal if she came back with my dad's graduation certificate, which is the equivalent of a high school diploma in the United States. *Kokojan* left their house angry, annoyed, and hurt from the rejection.

Two years would pass before *Kokojan* returned with a weapon that restored her ego and family honor: my dad's diploma. My mother says *Kokojan* quickly greeted the family at the door, and before she could be seated, she passionately slammed the graduation paperwork onto the coffee table for my grandfather's reading pleasure. It was no secret that she was back to finish the conversation she had started a couple of years prior. Because my grandfather was a man of his word, he agreed to the arranged marriage between my mom and dad.

At that time, my mother was 24 years old and "aging," but she was still an eligible bachelorette—otherwise known as an old maid in Afghanistan—so this was the appropriate next step in her life. She knew she would inevitably marry a man she hardly knew, but at least with this arrangement she wouldn't end up with a complete stranger. While she knew her days with her friends would come to an end, she understood the cultural norms and the expectations her family held of her. It was now a matter of honor and reputation to proceed with the decision according to her family's wishes. She wouldn't challenge her grandfather on a decision that had been made between the elders.

Years later, when Dad joked about the moment he "landed" my mom, he would say that his diploma was the result of multiple bribes to the teachers. His graduation paperwork was fake, but he needed something to prove that he had graduated high school. He would boast that Mom just could not help but to fall for his good looks and charm. Mom, unamused at his remarks, would roll her eyes and whisper some words under her breath. My dad and my siblings would all laugh at the way his version of the story always got a rise out of my mom. We loved watching our parents be romantic in their own strange way.

After my parents' wedding, the political situation in Afghanistan became worse. Imminent war with the Russians was about to break out in Kabul, and people either escaped it or became a casualty. My dad had joined the Afghan army, but civil unrest was brewing and he knew it was only a matter of time before it was him buried next to the soldiers who had already lost their lives. My parents were not only fearful for their own lives, but they were also worried about the life my mother was carrying inside of her body.

My grandmother, *Kokojan*, was the first to escape the war and arrive in America. She joined my older uncle who had come to the States in the early '70s to study horticulture. He underwent the lengthy process of visa sponsorship to declare refugee status for *Kokojan*, and once *Kokojan* had settled in with him, he began to focus on the paperwork that would eventually bring us to America.

5

Then There Was Me

Our beginnings in the womb of our mothers are not a matter of choice, but of destiny. The Russian invasion of Afghanistan forced my parents to move to Iran. I was born in Afghanistan as my parents left their country. My oldest cousin was with my mom during labor and present for my birth. She was also one of the nieces my dad had protected from the gunfire attack some years earlier. When I talk to my cousin about my birth, she remembers feeling helpless and frightened. She was a young, scared teenager when she was asked to support my mom during the most difficult time in her life.

Although it was a confusing situation for her at the time, my cousin and I laugh about how she was the first to hold me when I was born. To this day, we talk into the middle of the night while drinking green tea, reflecting on her experiences, and appreciating the importance of authentic connections within our own family dynamic. I can't help but feel an affinity toward her. "You should always listen to me, because I practically brought you into this world," she frequently says to me. Sometimes I wonder about all the events that connect me to my cousin, even those prior to the event of my birth. If Dad had not been there, would she have been met by bullets on the bus that day?

After my birth, my mom and dad made their way through Iran and into Pakistan. In the big cities of Iran, the buildings were architected progressively, the streets were clean, and the people were pleasant. Islamabad, Pakistan had the most beautiful gardens and parks, and the weather was warm enough for a daily stroll in the beautiful green park. Yet, no matter how nice Iran and Pakistan seemed, they were not Afghanistan; they were not *home*. No matter how my parents seemed to blend in with their looks, their accents and stories made it clear that they were foreigners.

My parents accepted their situation as a temporary one. They had planned to go back to Afghanistan when the war ended and raise their newborn daughter as an Afghan woman. Little did they realize, they had just begun their travels. Their world was changing for good, and even though they didn't fathom it until much later in life, my parents would call an entirely different place *home*.

My family entered Iran in hopes of finding a way to be with my uncle in America, but they were met with another form of political barrier. Because of the actions of Ayatollah Khomeini, the leader of the 1979 Revolution in Iran, political unrest between Iran and America was growing. Iranian rebels had taken American hostages, and as a result, Iran's relationship with the U.S. embassy was terminated. Refugees were no longer accepted through Iran, and the closest location for potential refugees was Pakistan, a neighboring country to the east. My parents understood the need to continue their travels, but decided to rest for a few months before making the trek across another country again.

Upon our arrival in Pakistan, I became really sick. My parents had been riding an old bus from Shiraz, Iran to Islamabad, Pakistan, and it was packed with fearful people in similar situations. The drive was long, bumpy, and dusty, exposing everyone to the elements. What I had wasn't the typical cold or flu. Mom says at one point I had both the whooping cough and measles all over my body, which made me cry during most of the bus ride. There were times that all my mom could see were little slivers between my puffy eyelids. My breathing was labored and my chest rose high with long intervals in between, leaving Mom feeling completely helpless.

During a very low moment, my mom broke down right there on the bus. With tears rolling down her face and the hot, flushed cheeks of her baby pressed against hers, she cried on my dad's shoulders and made a wish that we would just get someplace permanent. She wished that her little family would reach a safe place where she wouldn't have to wonder if she was going to live or die the next day. She wanted so badly to live in a home with a room she could place my tiny body in; a place that would let me heal. Instead, her child was suffering from breathing problems caused by inhaling the kicked-up dust of badly paved dirt roads. My mom's wishes were simple wishes any mother would understand. Convinced that I was going to die, she held onto me very tightly and prayed as we trekked across the country in the dusty, old bus.

Home of the Free and Brave

Through stories of dangerous bus rides, riding mules in the middle of the night, and walking long distances, I survived. My parents would eventually have four children: two boys and two girls. Many people call that perfection and worthy of the evil eye (yes, we believe that in our culture). While my parents started out living in the poorest parts of the San Fernando Valley and Los Angeles, they eventually moved to a nice suburb in California, which became the backdrop of most of my childhood.

My mom and dad became American citizens in order to create a stable life for us, as well as to keep us safe and together. The future of Afghanistan was looking more and more bleak every day, and the hopes my parents had about returning vanished with each setting sun. My parents didn't believe that renouncing their Afghan citizenship would make them any less Afghan; this thinking gave them peace of mind when they took their oath to become Americans. They knew the concept of the American value system promoted the freedom to raise their family the way they wanted to, as well as the opportunity to make a living using their skills and talents. America was far more safe and lucrative, and my parents understood it was necessary for their long-term survival to consider a more permanent vision for their family.

American-born citizens do not undergo the intense process immigrants go through to become naturalized citizens. Foreign-born candidates who choose naturalization after living in America for a few years are required to make a financial investment and submit an application. Over the course of many months or years of waiting, the candidates meet with immigration agents who administer various tests to determine if they can speak the English language, read the English language, and pass a basic civic and history test that most American-born citizens fail!

My parents somehow realized that it was an important part of our identity to be recognized as Americans instead of stateless individuals, so they started planting roots in the ground. My mother says that she and my dad studied together almost nightly for months before they took their tests with immigration agents. When they did become citizens, they made a point to vote in every election and didn't take for granted the freedoms that came with the privilege of living without the fear of death and war. Most of the issues my parents encountered regarding their American status were rooted in their fear of losing the rich cultural heritage that gave our family its identity in the first place.

Pancakes, Anyone?

My experience of being the first-born child in my family had a big impact on my character and personality. Not only was my place in the birth order a blessing and a curse, but I was also the guinea pig child in my family's cultural experiment. As with most kids who are the oldest in their family, I was the first pancake in the skillet—trying to be perfect, but completely misshapen with pieces of myself stuck everywhere and burns that can never be removed. I didn't completely understand this analogy until two things happened in my life. One, my father took us camping and I noticed that no one wanted to eat the first ugly pancake that came off the grill for breakfast. Two, although we grew up with the same parents, my siblings and I were nothing like each other. I was the first one to make a mistake and taught my siblings how to "avoid" being scolded at.

The part of being the first-born child that was a blessing pushed me become a natural leader in many different ways. I was far more responsible than any other kids I knew. By the age of 12, I was cooking for seven people, cleaning the whole house in an afternoon, and filling out all the school paperwork for me and my siblings. I didn't always appreciate being expected to do so much for my family. Sometimes if you listened close enough, you could hear me cursing my parents for all the chores I had to complete after school. My compliance (and ability to curse without being heard) kept me from getting into trouble, and I learned to work hard, delegate, and take charge of myself and others.

Conversely, the curse of being the oldest child meant that I had to be the first one to challenge my parents, take risks, or succumb to my family's desires. When the American culture I identified with didn't fit in with the "right" action my parents desired of me, I was the one who let all hell break loose for my family. My life from childhood to young adulthood became a constant game of red light, green light, often seeking approval from my parents. The worst thing my parents could say to me was, "She is turning into an American!" Only then did I realize how much trouble I was in.

As I write this, full circle and in the place of a parent, I often think about the curse words my kids use under their breath when they unwillingly participate in their daily chores. Raising children to be authentic Americans means accepting the strengths and weaknesses that come with the journey of dual-identities. While birth order plays a part in building character and personality, it becomes the responsibility of the parents to build an environment that provides space for curiosity and failure as necessary elements in the process of emotional maturity. The children and I often talk about the importance of heritage and our connection to our past, but I also convey that their responsibility is to be a contributing citizen of America. If they choose to build a bridge between their Afghan heritage and their American home for a better global community, that is their choice and a positive outcome of their natural born identities.

It took me a lifetime to realize that the most important lessons that form and shape our self-concept, or purpose in life, come from the messages we hear as children. While the journey of childhood doesn't always follow the fairytale and fantasy format we think it should, much of who we become as adults is shaped by how we perceive the world and the people living in it. As Multi-Americans, we are shaping the path for our children, and it is our responsibility to teach them to honor their heritage but to be the storyteller of their own lives.

6

The American Dream

On the outside, it appeared as though we were living the American Dream. Other Afghan families believed my parents had "made it" because we had a nice home and lived in a nice town. What they didn't realize is that my mom was working 60 hours a week and my dad was pulling 12 hours a night on the graveyard shift, running his own small business, and doing odd jobs in his spare time.

Many other Afghan families around us either moved from house to house, lived in government subsidized housing communities, or settled in run-down parts of town. Most people worked hard, but adjusting to life outside of Afghanistan was equally hard. We lived in a beautiful four bedroom, three bathroom home amidst other homes that looked the same—a symbol of the American

Dream. We were perfectly suburban and sat on top of a hill with a view from the backyard that overlooked a valley of rolling green hills and other perfect homes and communities.

Our home was located close to the beach, so my childhood memories are bursting with images and sounds of the weekends we spent on the California coastline. In fact, most of my childhood pictures consist of me on the beach, trying to show off my dark tan and curly, short hair. I would always don a half-smile in pictures in an attempt to prove I wasn't the troublemaker I appeared to be.

I remember doing a lot of traveling in our white minivan with the maroon fabric interior. We loved that car, and we only sold it because my baby sister had thrown up in it so much that there was a permanent smell coming from the carpet. When we were at home, I was usually in our backyard playing in the warm California sun. I didn't care about how I looked, and hygiene was not my priority. Brushing my teeth and washing my hands was a complete inconvenience to my playtime. I was always more interested in exploring the newest ant hill or bird's nest in our backyard. Playing in the dirt, climbing trees, and spending hours in the salty water of the beach were normal weekend activities for me. I flourished when I was in nature. My family knew I was most happy as a child when I was running around outside, turning the earth and ocean into my playground.

The Sleepover Games

My mom and dad were extremely protective of their children and didn't trust others to take responsibility for us. They tried hard to present an unadulterated view of the world by keeping us sheltered from its realities. Trust was not easily given to *anyone*, regardless of whether you were family or not. There were always fears that something terrible would happen to us; kidnapping, rape, and murder being the top three on the list of things that supposedly happen to Afghan children during sleepovers.

If you've ever tried arguing with an overprotective parent about the actual possibility of being raped or kidnapped over a sleepover, you know it's pointless. Mom would say, "If anything happened to you because I let you go, my life would be over." Our arguments and pleading did not stack up against the local news, which was one of the main accessible means for my parents to observe and understand American life. We wasted so much time as children trying to paint the picture that everything was fine.

However, whenever the sleepover debate shifted to staying with family, and the stars were aligned, we were sometimes successful. Persuading our parents to let us go became an art form that we developed over time. Whenever they said yes, we were so happy that you would think we had won the childhood lottery. But for us, this was an opportunity to finally hang out with our cousins, our only friends who really understood us.

Venturing away from our home to spend time with our cousins usually meant staying up for hours, playing board games, eating junk food, and talking about our American lives all night long. Sacrificing a night of sleep was a cheap price to pay to gain pure joy from being our authentic selves with each other. Sleepovers with American friends were out of the question, so we made the best of the opportunities we had.

Private Displays of Affection

Dad often showed Mom affection in our presence, and he made sure that we knew how important she was to him. Sometimes he would lift her up and carry her across the room while she was in the middle of washing the dishes. Mom would laugh and yell at Dad to put her down, as the dirty dishwater would drip from her hands to the floor. My siblings and I would gather around them and jump up and down so we could be included in the wrestling match that always turned into a tickle competition. Dad would pretend that we were strong enough to take him down, and we would all somehow end up on the floor laughing. We, the children of the family, were the center of the world he and my mother were creating in America. Not only was he the caretaker and protector of his family, but he was also the uncle in the family that everyone loved. My cousins all wished he was their dad. They still say that today.

While I didn't necessarily fear him on a day-to-day basis, I did fear the thought of doing anything he defined as "wrong" or "bad." (Now, I wouldn't call it emotional abuse, but Dad did once tell me he would murder me if I ever ran off with an American guy. It was in a joking manner, of course…Well, kind of.) Because I feared being seen as a disappointment in his eyes, the last thing I wanted was to defy or hurt him in any way. I felt an obligation to make him happy by becoming a perfect human being. While we all know that perfection is not possible, as a child I didn't see it that way.

Much of my identity was formed in this sort of fear-based thought process. It wasn't a very healthy way to live, but it was my way of coping with my surroundings and fitting in with my Afghan culture and identity. I grew up thinking my parents would only be happy if I was perfect, but trying to find the perfection of the American Dream while adhering to my Afghan roots proved to be very difficult.

Mother Tongue

Growing up, I spoke in my family's native tongue, but not without struggles. As children, we wanted to speak English all the time, but Dad had enforced a strict Dari policy at home.

He wasn't laid back about the idea either (as I am with my children today).

Once, my brother and I were playing, and one of us yelled, "I can run faster up the stairs than you can!" As if it were a movie, Dad suddenly appeared—wrinkled forehead and all—with the *Jaws* theme music announcing his entrance. The glare from his eyes cut straight through our souls like laser beams, causing us to immediately stop in our tracks. He didn't say much. He didn't have to. The sting of his laser beam eyes would stay with us for days or weeks at a time.

If we ever wanted to blurt something out in English, we would remember past burns and switch languages midway. The funniest part was struggling to remember how to say certain words in Dari, so we would speak "Darglish," our combination language of Dari and English. Sometimes when we felt rebellious, we would whisper to each other in English or Pig Latin, "Ahahay! Eythay illway evernay owknay atwhay eway areyay ayingsay!"

Mom was a little more relaxed than Dad when it came to speaking English at home. I believe she was supportive of it because she wanted to practice conversing with us. Her behavior was more indicative of assimilation into the American culture, so we didn't have to pretend with her. Mom never really yelled at us for not speaking Dari when Dad wasn't around, but of course, when Dad was around, she would say, "Speak Dari!" They both would tell us, "You will thank me one day," but it always seemed as though Mom was half as serious as Dad.

Mom was more passionate about literacy and our ability to read our mother tongue. Through the avenue of Sunday schools or personal lessons at home, she taught us how to read and write the Dari language. And let me just say, it was painful. We had to read backwards (from left to right), and there was a whole new set of letters to learn that could only be found in the books she carried with her. It was nothing like English. While I probably read like a first grader in the Dari language today, the point is I can read it! As painful as it was, I now appreciate having the foundational knowledge and ability to speak the Dari language. As a kid, I would have never admitted that.

Although it felt forced as a child, the truth is that children are able to grasp language skills much more successfully than adults. Numerous studies equate a child's brain to a sponge, so adding another language to my brain was not "hard on me" as a child. We simply did not want to be different. No one else we knew at school spoke Dari.

Too Cool for School

Speaking another language at home put us in the ESL (English as a Second Language) program at school, and that was *not* considered cool. Every year when the elementary or middle school registration forms would come out, they asked one question that made us lose all cool points with the other kids at school: "Does your child speak another language at home?" My parents proudly directed me to answered "yes" on the forms every single year.

Conceptually, ESL is a good program. It was created to help build the foundational knowledge a kid needs in order to be a successful communicator in America. The problem is that the program comes with the stigma of not appearing to be an authentic American. It was the little things—such as the separation from kids who didn't go to ESL or the smirks and laughs we heard when we were excused from the "normal class"—that bothered me. No matter how strong the personality, children remember moments when they feel like the outsider. They know when they are being made fun of or bullied. Most of us can relate, when we dig deep into our childhood memories and other unfortunate public cases that we have witnessed. The actions of other kids have an emotional impact on us, spanning from childhood through adulthood.

This tremendous gap between first generation children and our parents existed because our parents simply did not understand the social dynamics of being singled out in school. To them, rebellion against ESL classes appeared irresponsible and unreasonable. If we even tried to explain this concept to them, they would become angry at us. "If you are going to school and getting educated (for free in America), then why does any of this matter?" they would ask. Social acceptance was not a factor of success in our parents' eyes, and this was just one example of many other acculturation conflicts that would widen the gap between the generations.

Looking back as an adult, I understand that although we may have had our differences, being true to our authentic selves meant inclusivity for everyone. I did not feel included because I did not feel welcome to be myself in school. Unfortunately, authenticity was not a "cool" factor in the social dynamic of the American public school system I attended.

A New Way of Thinking

If the statement "the end justifies the means" holds true, then learning the Dari language has brought me so many benefits as an adult. For one, I was able to communicate with my grandparents and hear the stories of their lives before they passed on. Secondly, I could engage in conversation with relatives at family parties. Although it was difficult for me to speak the language with confidence, I found that the more I practiced, the more others saw me as a person invested in the learning process. I knew people cared when they corrected me. My uncles and aunts would listen to Afghan music during family gatherings and compliment me on my ability to understand what was being conveyed through the songs. As a result, I was able to connect to a whole new world of music and poetry. If there was ever a case for authentic interpretation of the arts, language was the first step to getting there.

As children, we didn't understand the importance of learning our mother tongue, but by increasing our ability to interact and communicate with more people in the world, we were being given the invaluable gift of human connection. Today, in working with Afghan refugee families, I realize how important it is to share the commonality of the language. Speaking Dari connects and binds us authentically because of how quickly we can talk about how to solve issues. Certain expressions or emotional words combined with hand gestures cause people to move physically and emotionally closer to you. The attention we command by speaking the same language sets us apart from those who do not have the capability of speaking the same language.

While I do not always speak Dari at home with my children today, they get practice speaking and writing it with their grandparents. The importance of human connection through language is such a strong value to me that my children have even attended a language immersion school in order to learn a third language in addition to Dari. The world is becoming smaller, and humankind is interconnected on many more levels in this age of information. The better we can bridge the gap between multiple cultures—though deliberate acts such as learning a foreign language—the better our chances of building tolerance and understanding toward each other as a species.

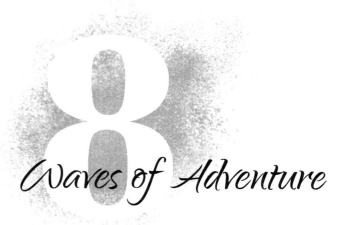

Waves of Adventure

Dad was an avid adventurer equipped with his own superhero car: the family minivan. Every weekend or spring break, he would drive us all over the West Coast, where no beach or national park went unexplored. Back then, crossing borders was not a worry for foreigners, so our family would frequently venture into Canada and Mexico as well. Sometimes our extended families would join us, and Dad would lead a caravan of cars toward unique destinations that none of us had visited before. He always insisted on being the one to plan the trips, and he usually paid for everything.

I loved the long family rides that took us through windy mountain roads because they gave me the opportunity to sit behind Dad and listen to him sing songs in Dari, even though I didn't completely understand them. Whenever we would go camping (and we went a lot), it was usually a huge family production. We would spend a few nights in a big, lime green tent with extended relatives who relied on my dad to show them a good time away from the harsh reality of living in big cities.

My fondest memories are of playing in the sands of unnamed beaches in Ventura County, California. In order to enjoy our space and privacy as a family, we never visited the crowded or named beaches. Upon finding a secluded beach, we would unpack our big blankets, bags of groceries, and our boombox. My family took up a lot of space, but that was okay because there was no one there to tell us to be more considerate or to quiet our loud voices.

Weekend trips to the beach usually meant we stayed outside in the sun all day. Sunblock was a foreign object to us. If we wanted sunblock, we either found some shade under a tree, or we would occasionally use an umbrella. Mom would typically pack us a wonderful, inconvenient meal like rice and chicken that would become seasoned with beach sand by the time it reached our mouths. We didn't care! We were so hungry we bit down on the grainy rice with pleasure.

Sometimes I would beg Dad to take me further into the ocean than I was allowed to go on my own. When he was in the mood and obliged our reckless demands, I would hold one of his hands with my brother usually hanging onto the other. As we approached the waves, we would dive under them and resurface, laughing and spitting out saltwater. Wave after wave would crash over us, yet we would move forward, enjoying the few seconds of calm before the next wave took us back underneath. We didn't give a second thought to dangers such as sharks, riptide currents, water temperature, or sometimes even 10-foot waves. Eventually, there would come a moment where I could no longer touch the ocean floor, but I would hold onto Dad's arm, trusting that he would keep me safe, no matter how far into the ocean we ventured.

Playing on the shores of the California beaches weekly gave me a darker skin tone, and my family soon gave me the nickname "*shawparki charmee*," directly translated from Dari to mean "bat," the little brown/black flying nocturnal creatures that use echo sonar powers to find and eat insects at night. My parents would laugh, and my father, who was lighter in skin tone than my mother, would laugh at me and say, "You got your *gandomi* [Dari for *wheat*] color skin from your mom." As a child I didn't care until I heard my extended family use the term in a derogatory way while laughing at me during a family dinner. Skin tone bias was something my family unconsciously associated with beauty, and something most other "brown" skinned people understand. The darker my skin turned with continued exposure to the sun, the uglier the names became. While I didn't stop playing in the sun altogether, I did sit in the shade more often as I grew into a young adult; my beliefs about beauty tainted by the worlds view on the shade of my brown skin color.

Part of My World

Remember the Scholastic Book Fair forms that teachers used to send home once a month with students in the '80s and '90s? I don't know about you, but for me, getting something from the book fair was the equivalent of receiving a long-awaited birthday gift. There is a secret I'm about to divulge that has been kept until this moment. When I was in the third grade, my uncle secretly bought me *The Little Mermaid* soundtrack on cassette tape. You might be wondering, *Why the heck does that matter?* or *What makes that worthy of 'secret' status?*

For one, the cost of *The Little Mermaid* soundtrack was a whopping five dollars. That was a lot of money for a third grader back then. I was sure my parents would say no because it was not a necessary expense…at least in their eyes it wasn't. Luckily, we had extended family living with us during that time, so I had a sympathetic eye witness to my first world problems.

That morning, after my Uncle Max had overheard me losing an argument with my parents about buying the cassette tape, he somehow convinced my parents to let him take us to school. Because he felt bad for me, he offered me money to pay for the cassette tape. While I was excited at the prospect of having my own *The Little Mermaid* soundtrack, I was hesitant about taking money from an older relative.

In the Afghan culture, it can be considered rude to accept money from older relatives if it is not a special occasion such as a birthday or religious holiday. The reason? If someone else is giving you money for something, the cultural interpretation is that your parents couldn't afford it, whatever "it" might be. Whether the money was available or not and whether or not that factor played a part in the decision-making process was beside the point. You just didn't go against your parents' wishes. No meant no, and we were not to push the matter any further once a final decision had been made. So, as a representative of my parents, it was my job to respectfully decline my uncle's offer, but I didn't want to. Boy, was I at a crossroads. Was this a joke or was I being set up?

I was scared that if I took the money and Dad found out, I would be punished. Uncle Max, a rebel in many ways himself, observed me as I began sweating and twitching around in the passenger seat of his red Yugo hatchback. I was mentally preparing a "Darglish" version of my declination speech, when Uncle Max relieved my anxiety by being the first to fill the silence. He leaned over like a mob boss and whispered, "I promise I won't tell your parents. Just take this." *What?* I thought to myself. *Did I hear him correctly?*

Looking me straight in the eyes, he forcibly placed the crisp five-dollar bill into my tiny hands. My eyes widened and my jaw dropped. I remember thinking that I had either just hit the jackpot or I was on my way to an adolescent meltdown in front of my parents later that day. Not wanting to upset the mob boss, I hesitantly agreed to the deal. I knew that as long as Uncle Max kept his end of the bargain and didn't rat me out, I could ride off into the sunset with my *The Little Mermaid* soundtrack like Thelma and Louise.

Anxiously, I walked into my classroom and submitted the money and the form, on which I had forged my parent's signature. I was a criminal getting away with cultural murder. Six weeks later, when I received the cassette tape from my teacher, I treated it like a national treasure. After all, if anyone found the tape, it had the potential to destroy my childhood glee. I removed anything that made the cassette tape stand out or look unique, then I stashed it among the many other tapes that I had collected in my room. After holding my breath for so long, I could finally exhale. Life was good for a moment. My criminal behavior had gone unnoticed, and I could finally move on to enjoying my next daydream rendezvous. Rebellion never felt so good.

As a mermaid cursed with two legs instead of a fin, I would sit on the handcrafted swing my father had built in our backyard and push my legs as high as they would take me. Staring at the sky while I was swinging was one of my favorite childhood pastimes. I would pretend that it was the water, and I believed that if I went just fast enough, my swing would flip over and I would turn into a mermaid and be back under water where I actually belonged. When the swing couldn't go any higher, I would jump into the air and land as far as I could. Most people imagined themselves flying, but I imagined myself floating through water.

When I was done swimming around in the crabgrass and dirt of my backyard, I would step into the house and instantly return to reality. To my mother's displeasure, I would leave a trail of mud throughout the house; evidence that I had been in her beloved garden eating away at the fruits or vegetables of her labor. Trailing mud in the house was also evidence of my careless mannerisms and hatred of being neat and tidy; a trait disliked by most parents. Mom would give me one look and direct me to go back outside and leave my sandals on the patio. I was too lazy to wash them off with the hose before coming back in, so they were usually added to the pile of mud-ridden flip-flops the sun had baked into a small, crusty mountain.

As a child, my identity crisis manifested itself in the fantasy worlds I created, and I relished in the fact that my imagination could take me far from where I wasn't sure I belonged. Becoming a mermaid was freeing, because I didn't have to be American or Afghan. I was an entirely different creature that couldn't fit into a box or be checked off on a census. They say children are resilient, and while I believe this is true, children are also capable of experiencing and internalizing emotions like loneliness and fear. The constricting culture of our family dynamic created many opportunities for me to create multiple imaginary identities. I am pretty sure I became a mermaid again later in my life when I took my first ride on a motorcycle.

Food for Thought

Food is a big deal in Afghan culture. Nourishment is not only necessary for the body, but it also brings sustenance to the soul. I know most cultures have a love for food, as evidenced by the existence of the Food Network channel, but it is a borderline obsession for us to get together and stuff our faces as a family.

Afghan families typically prepare meals "family style," with various dishes consisting of meat, rice, and salad spread across the table for the taking. Sharing love for Afghan food was, and still is, one of the most common reasons people in my culture came together in America. The women who loved to cook and express their creativity through culinary art were usually blessed (or cursed) to be busy with family events on the weekends. During the casual planning conversations between families, those with less than desirable cooking skills were usually not asked to host. Afghan food has a way of bringing people together, which makes it one of the gifts of my culture that is precious beyond measure.

Mom always shared her home-cooked meals with our neighbors and her coworkers. It was her way of sharing her cultural identity in complete authenticity. She was proud of her neighborhood fame, and though she always pretended to act modest when she would receive compliments, I knew she was beaming inside. She was most famous for her "Kabuli Palau," a combination dish with caramelized spice-infused rice, pieces of chicken, and a beautiful presentation of raisins and carrots sprinkled on top. People would comment on how talented a cook she was or how they had heard about her food from "so and so," and that made her and my family proud.

Large family dinner parties were the norm and most of the time, my uncles, aunts, and cousins were present for the feast. The smells that would come from the kitchen were a cause for celebration in and of themselves. The combination of onions, chicken, rice, and exotic spices would wake the neighbors from their boring lives and have them venture to our door to ask, "What is that smell? Can we have some?"

When we didn't have to entertain large amounts of people on the weekends, we usually ate simpler meals. Although in Afghan culture it wasn't typical for the husband to cook for the family, if Mom was too busy working extra hours on the weekend, Dad would bake fresh flatbread and seasoned chicken drumsticks for us to eat with whatever fresh vegetables we picked from our garden. Dad had the hands of a chef, so everything he cooked tasted delicious. My brother, baby sister, and I would sit on the floor next to my dad while he ripped apart tiny pieces of bread—enough to fit between two of our fingers—and placed them on the *distarkhan* (a special piece of cloth laid out on the floor made specifically for eating on). Then he would fill our cups with sweet tea, milk, or good old-fashioned Coca-Cola, and we would sip on our beverages until we'd have to hold our cups high to let the final drops trickle into our mouths. Then, of course, we'd ask for more.

Even though we loved eating with our father, we never talked about it with our friends at school. We thought it was weird. No one else we knew ate on the floor, let alone had a special cloth for such meals. Thankfully, no one could find out about it because we had two large dining tables in our house like other normal American families. In fact, one was so fancy that we never used it, as it was covered with clear plastic during the weekdays.

The Beef with Food and Family

As kids, we didn't always appreciate the fact that our meals were fresh and made from scratch. Forget about the value of sharing meals together; we were too young to really appreciate all of that. All we wanted was to eat at McDonald's. After all, it was what all the kids at school talked about. The healthy, fresh food and the rice and meat meals were getting old. We just wanted to be like our friends who ate fast food at least three times a week. Whenever our parents would agree to take us to McDonald's, I wouldn't care that I wasn't allowed to pick what I wanted. I would just politely eat my cheeseburger knowing that it was a treat, considering how expensive it was to feed our family of six. What mattered to me most was that I was like the others for a moment. I felt validated and normal.

Family dinners were only appealing to me at that time in my life because I got to hang out with other kids like me; cousins close to my age. Unlike the adults, we stayed away from the talk about politics and arguments over what was happening in Afghanistan. When politics became too heated of a topic or when feelings were getting hurt between friends, they would switch to the subject of religion. When that topic got old, they would complain about how kids were too rebellious, not acting Afghan enough, or becoming "lost" to the American culture. The parents often gave each other advice on how they would handle such situations, but the fear was evident on all of their faces. They were worried that their own kids would fall into the same traps and bring their family dishonor.

The conversation inside the house always seemed boring to us, so we would beg to go outside to either play baseball with the neighbors or walk to a nearby park. We wanted to play in the world we had created for ourselves, not the world of chatter our parents existed in. Once we were in a safe zone away from the parents, we would talk about how our parents were unfair for not letting us go to sleepovers or birthday parties with our American friends. Hesitantly, we would share that we liked boys from our classrooms, knowing that we would never act on the impulse to tell someone we thought they were cute.

Sometimes when the cousins would get mad at each other or develop different "cliques," we would bring up the secrets that had previously been shared in confidence. Then, we would black-mail each other and threaten to tell each other's parents. While it never happened, the idea of having all your secrets revealed felt like an earth-shattering self-destruct button. The problem was that all the cousins had one of these buttons, so you were careful not to push someone else's button unless you yourself were ready to self-destruct.

Even though we recognized our differences, we bonded be-cause we did not have to explain to each other why we were the way we were. It was as authentic as relationships could get, and we were lucky that family dinners brought us together almost ev-ery weekend.

10

Black Sheep

My parents, like other Afghan diaspora who had come to America, were afraid of exposing us to strangers who didn't understand the Afghan culture and ways. For that reason, I was never watched by the neighborhood babysitter. I never had a nanny. I never went to daycare. I was closely guarded within the walls of our own Afghan community. Being the overprotective parents they were, my parents insisted on working opposite shifts so that one of them could always be home with us. There were, however, a couple of hours a day where I was the head of the household; right after Dad left for his evening shift and before Mom returned home from work.

While watching my siblings was not that difficult, it did place a lot of pressure on a hormonal preteen who wanted to be with her friends instead of making Hershey's chocolate syrup sandwiches for her siblings. I took care of my siblings almost every day for those few hours after school, and it shaped me into a natural caretaker of people. Being the mother of five children that I am today, I attribute my ability to stay sane to the fact that I was an engaged participant of a large family with complex issues.

People often ask me, "How do you do it? How do you deal with five kids?" I wonder if they're asking because I have a career or because I should look more exhausted. The question is loaded with assumptions that I do not have an elevator pitch for, but I can say that there is no shortage of love or support in our household. This does not mean that it's not a production when we go somewhere together, but being a natural caretaker means my children know they can lean on me for support, the way my siblings did when we were home alone.

The protective nature of my parents became more inconvenient for me as I grew into my preteen years. When I started interacting with other girls at school, they would usually ask me to come over to their houses after school. The usual response from my parents was, "No. We don't know who they are. They can come here, but you are not allowed there." The truth was that it didn't matter if my parents "knew" the family or not. This was their way of preserving their culture and minimizing the influence others might have had on us. The intentions of our parents, however innocent, created a bigger gap between the commonalities we shared with them.

Liking boys, listening to rock or rap music, and sharing emotions were not considered normal behavior for Afghan girls. True to human nature, we still did all these things without our parents' knowledge. I was becoming more American and less Afghan, and I knew my parents wouldn't like that, so I hid it. Those who were labeled as a black sheep were sent to the slaughterhouse of relationships where their parents would disown them. I didn't want to think about a world without my parents. I was emotionally dependent on their love, even if it meant that I could only show half of myself.

Don't Open the Garage

I grew up in an agricultural area that consisted mostly of migrant Mexican families in the valley and rich white people in the hills. I don't know how my parents swung it, but we ended up in a nice neighborhood on the more affluent side of town. We were clearly the only brown people on our street, and it showed in more than just our skin color.

Our family always had at least six cars in the driveway, with three of the cars being a "work in progress" until Dad would get fed up with the oil spills in the driveway and sell the run-down cars for less than what he paid for them. Quicker than the rate of exchange on the previous project, the money would burn a hole in his pocket, driving him to buy another car that he would park in our driveway. A few months later, the vehicle would either be sold or its insides would be taking up space in the garage.

As my family's makeshift lawyer, I would always respond to the complaints of the HOA by making false promises to move the junk off the driveway. That usually did the trick for a few months until someone complained again and we had to undergo another monthly inspection by the committee.

As if we didn't stand out enough, Afghan folk usually travel in packs, like wolves. A typical Afghan family usually consists of four to six people, but with multiple families joining us for dinner on the weekends, there were always strange-looking people coming in and out of our home. The women wore scarves on their heads and the men were loud, hairy, and boisterous. We greeted our guests for what seemed like hours on the doorsteps, usually driving up the noise to pollution levels for our cookie-cutter suburban neighborhood. At night, the same enthusiasm would ensue on our doorsteps as our guests would leave our home. Looking back, we were the black sheep of the neighborhood, but there was a herd of us, so it did not feel so lonely or ostracizing.

11

Unapologetic Matriarch

Kokojan lived with us until the day she passed away. Not only was she *not* a normal-looking American, but she also dressed in very traditional Afghan clothes. Her outfit usually consisted of a large, pastel-colored dress that she coupled with baggy white-laced bottoms. A traditional white *chadoor* (a thin Afghan-style head covering), wrapped around her white and silver shoulder-length hair that was always braided in the back. When her health allowed, she would take walks in our front yard in full view of the whole neighborhood.

All of the neighbors stared at her, but she held her head high. She was old, but she was strong and commanded respect from anyone who interacted with her. "Hi" and "good" were the only English words she really knew, so when the neighbors were friendly, she would smile, wave, and greet them with "hi." When they asked how she was doing, she would reply, "Good." I always imagined that she walked with a trail of light behind her, as if angels were showering her with blessings.

Kokojan was the matriarch of our family and very religious. She had travelled to Mecca, Saudi Arabia to perform the religious pilgrimage many times, and she spent most of her time—even into the late hours of the night—in constant ritual prayers or reading the Quran. She kept all of her worldly possessions inside her bedroom over the stairs; her sanctuary. On the weekends, when she was surrounded by family, my dad and uncles would lay down on big, red mats reminiscing with her about the past or discussing some other family affair.

When she wasn't praying or reading the Quran, *Kokojan* would sit on her bed and watch her favorite American TV shows, *Three's Company* and *Bewitched*. We would often hear her laugh out loud at the main character, Jack Tripper, when he would make loud noises or get slapped by one of his two female roommates for requesting a threesome. Watching those shows as an adult, I realize that she must not have understood the sexual and sexist humor in the dialogue, or else she would have been offended and prayed for their dirty souls. *Kokojan* rarely came downstairs because it was physically difficult for her. As long as we weren't murdering each other while my parents were at work, we wouldn't see or hear from her. Everyone was happier that way.

Kokojan never embraced my mother. They had a typical *aroos-khooshoo* (bride and mother-in-law) relationship that usually put my dad in the middle of their arguments. I never witnessed first-hand the fights between Mom, Dad, and *Kokojan*, but the tension between the two women created the impression that my mom was never good enough in her mother-in-law's eyes. It did not matter that *Kokojan* was living in my mother's home; Mom was just the daughter-in-law who existed solely to serve her husband and in-laws. *Kokojan* saw me as a protective extension of my mom, so naturally, I was not on the winning side of the battle.

Don't Get Caught with the Almond Roca

Unfortunately, I was merely an observer in the life and story of *Kokojan*. Not a fan of my excessive energy or childish shenanigans (something she made very clear with her eyes), *Kokojan* only knew me to be a wild child that would sneak into her room without her permission. In times of exhaustion or bad health, she would ask me to make her lunch or dinner. She would give me strict instructions from the top of the stairs, reminding me to mix half a cup of rice with frozen mixed veggies and one chicken drumstick in a small stovetop pot—no salt and no oil. She was on a restricted diet due to her failing heart and cholesterol issues. I would bring her food up to her on a small white plate, and she would nod in appreciation if the food met her standards. When I burnt her food, she would look at me the way she looked at my mom.

When *Kokojan* appeared happy, that was my cue to start talking about cats. She liked cats, and that was the only thing I could find that I had in common with her. During the time that we had a cat of our own, before Mom made it disappear, I would bring it to *Kokojan's* room for her to pet. She would talk about how Muhammad, the great prophet of Islam, loved cats because they were very intelligent creatures. After a few minutes, I would run out of cat facts and there would be an awkward silence—my cue that it was time to go.

Kokojan kept a small fridge in her room that was stocked with fruit-flavored yogurt. Sometimes, when she was fast asleep or in the bathroom, I would sneak into her room and steal one of her yogurts. She also kept Almond Roca candy and lots of money under her gigantic, fancy bed. Being a troublemaker, I would take all sorts of things from her. Although she never caught me, I assume her lack of affection for me was also an indicator that she knew about my kleptomania.

I continued to steal into my tween years, and not just from *Kokojan*, but from many retail stores as well. I enjoyed the thrill of it and didn't think about the moral consequences of taking something that didn't belong to me. Evading the moral complexities that came with stealing, I considered myself to be a pirate collecting treasure.

Over time, I realized that stealing was bad, so I stopped. Even so, I was learning to sweep my mistakes under the rug, so I didn't see the point in disclosing my shortcomings to my parents. Though I was surrounded by love and guidance, I felt so alone at times, and the adrenaline rush of stealing couldn't fix that ever-widening hole inside of me. There wasn't enough delicious Almond Roca in the world to fill it.

Ladies and Gentlemen, Boys and Girls

The adults in my family, including my extended relatives, were a bit ethnocentric. According to them, the Afghan way of doing things was right and the American way of doing things was wrong. Our culture was and continues to be full of double standards between males and females, with females usually receiving the shorter end of the proverbial "independence stick." Ask any first- or second-generation Americans who have come from immigrant families, and they will share similar stories of gender roles and expectations.

Most cultures around the world restrict the role of women to being a family caretaker. I have even heard the following statement from some Afghan elders (roughly translated from Dari): "A woman is like a white piece of cloth. Whatever happens to her is visible and stains not only her, but everyone knows it and sees it. Because of that, we need to be careful with our women." What did that make boys then? A dark piece of cloth that never picked up any stains? What's with the cloth reference to begin with? I had so many questions, but I resigned myself to refrain from asking them.

My siblings and I went to school like normal American children, although it never felt normal to me. When someone would ask me where I was from and I would say Afghanistan, they would reply with, "Africa?" Everyone except for my fourth grade teacher, who was a hippie who had gone to Afghanistan for leisure in the 1970s, would respond like that to me. She was my favorite white person in the world, and even wore her Afghan dress on Halloween that year to pretend she was the Afghan queen, and I was the princess. Not many of my future teachers could stack up to Ms. Pinson, my adopted white Afghan Queen.

Other educators were hit or miss, and it was up to me to build a relationship with them. My parents didn't go to open house nights unless the teachers called to invite them, or for some reason a teacher took an interest in planning for my future. Most teachers assumed I was Mexican and tried to speak to me in broken Spanish. There was always a surprised look on their faces when I spoke back in perfect English. Some responded positively by asking where I was from, and others sat me at a table with all the other brown children and hardly interacted with us.

The last year in elementary school, the school decided to headline the great musical *Fiddler on the Roof,* a story about a Russian man named Tevye living with his three daughters as a Jewish family in the early 1900s. My homeroom teacher, a small Jewish lady with curly black hair and thick glasses, was the producer of the play, and this was going to be the show of a lifetime for her. After two days of high stakes drama club tryouts, Brandi, Sarah, and Emily were offered the three leading roles of the daughters. It was through no fault of their own, as they were beautiful girls who couldn't help but beam beauty from their lovely blonde or ginger hair, beaming blue eyes, and perfect freckles. The rest of us ended up in the dark section behind the stage known as the "chorus" group. It was never Shahira, Alejandra, Yolanda, Guadalupe, or Alma that were offered leading roles, even though there were more of us and we were full of character and chatter. Not one brown child had a leading or visible supporting role, and not one person in the establishment saw this as a problem. As I grew older, it was these unspoken truths that made me feel second class as a brown person.

Though I knew perfect English, I was always placed in the ESL classes, so most of my friends were from Mexico. The combination of spending most of my days at school with people who were not like me and seeking to be perfect in the eyes of my parents resulted in the development of multiple identities. I kept my wild and loud persona at school with friends, and my quiet, good girl persona stayed at home with my family. My teachers sent home notes saying that I was a distraction to other students because of my social butterfly tendencies in class, and my parents kept threatening to come to my school and sit with me if it happened again. It was becoming more and more clear that social genius was not a valued asset for a little lady in my position, so I played along with whatever crowd I was with at the time. More imperatively, I learned to shut my mouth when the teachers were looking.

Flipping Close to the Sun

Being an athletic person in elementary school, I often beat the boys in any sport. I was the champion of neighborhood baseball, and if I wasn't already the captain, I was always the first to get picked to join a team. Sometimes I would hit the ball so hard that it would end up halfway down the block, giving the kids on the opposite team a run for their money.

As a certified daredevil, I would walk up the rail of stairs in the living room and jump from the second-floor railing onto the couches on the first floor, just for the thrill of it. My audience of siblings and cousins would watch in amazement, sometimes injuring themselves when they tried to imitate me. Fear of heights or bodily harm never crossed my mind because I had done it so many times that I thought I was invincible. I even made myself believe that I could jump off of my roof and fly. Using a plastic trash bag as my parachute, I learned the hard way that I was not a bird or an airplane.

I became so rambunctious that Dad eventually turned our backyard swing into a monkey bar. That was where I learned how to do "cherry drops," a backwards flip off of the monkey bars which usually ended in a perfect landing for me. When I started climbing the refrigerator to find the chocolates Mom hid from us, then flipping off the top of the fridge to the ground, my parents knew they had to find a better outlet for my excessive energy levels. If nothing more, they needed to save their fixtures and furniture from my destructive behavior. After some research, Dad quickly enrolled me in gymnastics, a sport fitting to all my natural abilities—much better than the sport of couch destroying I was going to win a gold medal (and a scolding) for.

Gymnastics allowed me to develop balance, flexibility, and strength as a young girl. I was not afraid to take chances, and it showed on the mat. In a short few months, I excelled at levels beyond anyone's expectations, and I was having a blast. During practice one day, I saw my coach pull my parents aside to talk to them. I wasn't sure what they were discussing, but I could see all of them looking back at me. Being an extreme show off, I did my first double flip to demonstrate my skills. Nailed it. I was expecting clapping and a thumbs up from my dad, but surprisingly, my parents and coach didn't respond to me. Was I that bad? Should I have done a fancier trick? Unfortunately, that day was my last in a formal gymnastics class.

I was devastated, but quickly bounced back and returned to my household Olympic games. All I knew was that my parents couldn't take me to gymnastics anymore, but I didn't question their decision. *Maybe they couldn't afford it*, I thought to myself, shrugging off any other serious thoughts about it.

Later in life, when I spoke to my mom about the discussion that happened with my coach that day, I discovered that my coach was urging my parents to sign me up for Olympic training classes. While this would be considered the highlight of some people's dreams, my parents declined the coach's offer, causing a dismal ending to their meeting. Dad and Mom had discussed the situation and come to the conclusion that they didn't want their Afghan daughter tumbling around in public wearing nothing but underwear. Nope, not on their watch! From then on, I was no longer enrolled in any other extracurricular sports, as I suspect my parents didn't want to test those waters again.

Mom and I often laugh together when we discuss this defining moment in the life of little Shahira. I tease her about the fact that I could have been a gold medal Olympian hanging out with all the best like Mary Lou Retton, who was my idol at the time. My short, stocky build couldn't have been a more perfect fit for gymnastics, and my parents could have used the prize money to buy new couches for the living room.

Today, we both acknowledge the silly but real consequence of living within the strict boundaries of culture. In this case, it resulted in a huge missed opportunity for me. We debate about why it was a wrong decision or why it was a right one, but the fact is that most Afghan or Muslim girls would probably find the same fate today. The female body is a huge topic of focus within our religion and culture, and to my parents, putting it on display was not a decision they could agree to.

As a parent of three daughters today, there is a lot of discussion in our household around playing sports, how to dress, and what it means to "dress modestly." While I am not strict on my daughters about how they dress, I reiterate the importance of modesty as a value beyond external appearances. When my teenage daughter wore a short skirt-dress at a family event, she was approached by multiple males in the extended family expressing concern for "showing" her legs. This is an expected response from a cultural standpoint, so I was not surprised. As a mother, I chose to validate her by giving her permission to be confident about her choice of dress. I chose to validate her by telling her that she was beautiful because of who she was and not because of what she was wearing.

Additionally, I encourage my daughters and my sons to play whatever sports they are interested in because it's important to their development and health as human beings. Wearing shorts, tank tops, or uniforms are not even part of the conversation when it comes to sports. The truth is, when my children leave home to become independent adults, they will dress in whatever manner they want. Teaching the value of internal modesty and sanctity of the human body is the real lesson, and it is something my children hear from me often.

Fighting Spirit

When he wasn't playing with us at night, Dad was watching his favorite boxers—Evander Holyfield, Mike Tyson, and George Foreman—go at it in the heavyweight class. In 1997, when Mike Tyson bit Evander Holyfield's ear off in the Vegas showdown, my dad talked about it for weeks. Even he was victim to media gossip, if the glove fit. No matter where I was in the house, I would often hear him cheering in the living room. If his favored opponent was winning or losing, you would know it based on the tone of his deep voice.

Some days he would engage me or my brother in boxing matches. We had a pair of red sparring gloves and used the couch pillows to practice our punches. (I know what you're thinking... hadn't the couches taken enough punishment from my daredevilry?) Mom would yell at Dad to stop teaching me how to fight because I was an Afghan girl and it was inappropriate, but he would ignore her and continue yelling, "Jab, jab, jab!" The boxing lessons he gave us were never serious for long though, because my siblings or I would end up wrestling him to the floor. It was more fun pretending to bite his ears off and watch as laughter spread throughout the entire household.

I am sure that in the back of his mind, Dad was trying to establish connections with us that he hoped would stay with us for the rest of our lives. He wanted his home to always be our paradise on earth, so that we would never have to separate as a family. After all, if he could be our father as well as our friend, we would not want or need to seek a life outside of the safe world he had created for us. We would not need the approval of others. We would only require his and my mom's approval.

13

Kind of, Sort of, Maybe Me

When I was with my parents, I was a certified, organically grown Afghan girl merely living in America. At home, my family called me by my middle name, Niggin. At school, I went by Shahira. While I cannot say that I could have been diagnosed with dissociative or multiple personality disorder, I can say that I experienced a mild disassociation between who I was at home and who I was outside the home. Both names represent the same person in the mirror today; however, I did not believe that when I was younger.

Family members who chose to break traditions were causing widespread panic among the rest of us. We began asking questions like, "Why can't Auntie marry an American guy?" or "Why did my cousin run away from home?" "Why aren't we allowed to talk to her or go to her house anymore?" Mom and Dad were having a hard time answering our questions, which weren't cute anymore now that we were teenagers.

My father was extremely strict in enforcing the "isolation of the wrongdoer" rule when someone would break cultural norms. When a couple of my aunts were young adults, they dated American men. Although dating was always done in secret, sometimes the rebels in the family were caught in public with strange looking men. When my dad found out, he made it clear that my aunts were no longer welcome at our house. He insisted that Mom break ties with her family because he didn't want his children exposed to a setting where these circumstances (a.k.a. dating American men) were viewed as acceptable. Not wanting to rock the boat, Mom would agree with Dad to appear compliant. My mother's trips to my maternal grandparents' house were usually made alone without my dad. He didn't know it, but my mother still saw her sisters and maintained her relationship with them. Sometimes, when we would tag along on those trips to my maternal grandparents' home, Mom would urge us not to tell Dad that we had seen our aunts there. It created a huge psychological distance between us and my mom's family. Since they were not good enough for Dad, we didn't develop very deep connections with them. The pride and severity of ostracizing someone usually lasted a lifetime.

The Stonewalling of Billy Joel

Out of genuine fear that we would leave our roots, my parents kept looking for ways to stay connected with us. They did strange things that I considered dumb, like loudly singing American songs with an obvious Dari accent. Yup, we sang Billy Joel's "In the Middle of the Night" together anytime we were in the car for an extended amount of time. It was Dad's favorite American song, and singing it with him made us feel as close to him as he did to us in those moments. The song would play on repeat until everyone was sick of it.

As a preteen, there were some days that I didn't want to admit I was having fun, while other days I would dig my head in my hands and put on my famous sourpuss frown. Sometimes my parents would yell at me for having an attitude, but I was good at punishing them by keeping up the act up for long periods of time.

It was not a mature thing to do, but I became a pro at stonewalling my family for days on end. Stonewalling became a habit, and I did it every time I didn't get my way at home, and sometimes even in school. When I was going through a major battle in my head, like *Billy Joel is not cool, and listening to the same songs as my parents means I am a lame nerd, even if I do like them,* I would refuse to speak or participate for hours. I wanted to blast Sisters With Voices (SWV) on my portable CD player and ignore my family, but they would yell at me for not participating and take my small music contraption away from me. That would make me even angrier, causing my stonewalling routine to last for days.

As if the teen years are not a mess in and of themselves, with all the hormones and physical body changes, the mid '90s brought the most difficult of life's challenges to my family. Our experiences in the next decade shaped our individual and family identities more than any other. While we did not know it at the time, Dad had been battling cancer for years. When I hear Billy Joel now, I think of Dad. My guard is down, my heart is open, and the emotional walls that I had built up over the years are nothing but rubble. But the crumbling of walls took time, and as far as this story is concerned, there are more bricks to be broken down.

14

Dad's Kryptonite

I was about 12 years old when my mom shared with me that my dad, the strongest man alive, had been diagnosed with colon cancer. Cancer? No, that could not be correct. Either she had heard incorrectly or the doctors didn't know what they were saying. Prior to that moment, I wasn't sure of all the details, but I had figured that he was sick when he and my mom started going away for long hours on the weekends. Once family dinners stopped, we all knew something had changed.

Only now does Mom hesitantly speak of the many trips to the bathroom with my dad where he would empty pools of blood from his diseased colon. Initially, she cried for weeks because he refused to see a doctor; however, constant nagging from her led him to see a professional. He was undergoing mini biopsy surgeries every month, but somehow my parents managed to hide the seriousness of the situation from us. Even then, my dad was a human shield, this time emotionally absorbing the fear and pain of his family.

Sometimes Dad would yell or scream for Mom because he was in so much pain, and my siblings and I would sit on the stairs watching her run up and down for medical supplies. When Mom did catch a glimpse of our scared and curious faces, she would shut the bedroom door behind her. It would be hours before she would come out again. As children, we measured the seriousness of the situation by how many Disney movies we could watch before seeing them again.

It wasn't long before Dad's loud cries became a normal part of the day. If there was Jell-O or ice cream sitting next to the lamp on his nightstand, we knew that he was really sick and would be in bed for days. Sometimes I couldn't help but wear my sadness, confusion, and concern on my face. In those moments, Dad would change my dreary disposition by sharing his treats with me. For a moment we could pretend that he was fine and everything was like it used to be.

Unfortunately, cancer was not the only storm my family was weathering. Because Dad's illness made him weak, he could not perform more traditional jobs that required eight to twelve hours of his time. His options were limited to focusing on his small business of recycling printer cartridges, which wasn't very profitable. Financial troubles were on the horizon, making their way toward the shore. Little did we know, a storm was about to pass through our lives.

Money Is No Object

Dad was what you would call an avid entrepreneurial type. Sometimes he would spend the mortgage on money making ideas that would never pan out. Impulse buys such as fishing boats or cars seemed like a good deal, until they broke down. Because he could never resell them for more than what he paid, it wasn't a lucrative business model. As kids, we played along because finances were not our worry and there were always plenty of adventures with Dad. He always wanted to give us more and often went into debt doing so.

Dad didn't have great credit, but when he was given money, he found a way to spend it on his family. Mom, on the other hand, knew we were on the Titanic and could see the iceberg of financial disaster ahead, but her warnings weren't enough to stop him. Her voice of reason was usually silenced since Dad was the one who made the final call on all big spending decisions. To further complicate matters, Mom's emotional state enabled him to justify whatever wacky or unreasonable purchase he wanted to make. Why would our financial state matter if his days on earth were limited?

When I was 13, my mob boss Uncle Max moved to Colorado with my grandparents. Uncle Max would call and rave about how wonderful and affordable it was to live in Colorado, and he strongly encouraged our family to move there. There was a promising life in Colorado and soon enough, my Dad began to formulate a very different vision for our family.

Speechless

Some moments are so vivid that the images they create in my mind's eye never go away. As Dad was telling me about our move to Colorado, the painter inside my brain began to create. Imagine a nighttime scene with a dark green mountainous valley and dark grey clouds in the background. If you look closely, you can spot a tiny cabin nestled inside of one of the valleys with candle lights flickering inside and a trail of grey smoke rising from the chimney, slowly dissipating into the cold valley. We were moving toward a state of darker colors and further isolation, away from the bright yellow California sun and the deep blue ocean where I had spent so much time.

Sometimes I think my parents knew that I was turning into a rebellious teen behind the scenes. Mom says that she and Dad were afraid of me turning into a typical "American girl." They associated my behavioral changes with being in California, a place that had become the epitome of bad: bad finances, bad illnesses, and bad influences on the children. I was a confused 14-year-old who had spent her entire lifetime people-pleasing and investing in a second identity. All the false stories about my fancy lifestyle had made me popular, and the cool kids were just starting to take notice. Dad put a screeching halt on my master plan to fit in, and my raging hormones only added fuel to the fire.

I thought I knew it all and contemplated running away with my older, more rebellious cousins. Even though I knew I would never go through with it, I would still fantasize about making it on my own. My parents were convinced that they would be safer in Colorado, and somehow everything would work out. I didn't feel that way at all. I didn't want a new life. I didn't want new friends or to have to go to a new school where I didn't know anyone. I had never felt so angry and hopeless. My parents had made up their minds about turning our life completely upside down, and as usual, we weren't consulted about any of it.

In haste, the picture-perfect suburban dream house that we loved so much was sold, and we were on our way to a much smaller house in one of the northern suburbs of Colorado. My mom had the hardest time adjusting because she had lost the most in the move. The beautiful house that she had worked so hard to make her own was no longer hers. Moreover, Mom had become a successful business analyst, making good money and a name for herself. All of the hours she had worked and her commitment to her job resulted in an actual career in the healthcare industry. Just as I was working so hard to fit in, she had been doing the same in her own ways. Because Mom knew she couldn't support our family solely on her income, she went along with my dad's impulsive decision to leave. This was goodbye all over again.

15
Welcome to Colorado

Mom could have cared less about our new house, and it showed in the way that she chose not to decorate or do any yard work like she had done at our old house. To make matters worse, Dad's extravagant spending habits hadn't changed, and we found ourselves taking out loans that we couldn't afford to pay back. In an attempt to make up for bad financial decisions, we sold our small house in Colorado, but this time the consequences were insurmountable, and we couldn't buy another house. Rentals and moving from house to house became a way of life.

Like my dad, Mom became a human shield, protecting us from the financial storm that threatened to overtake us. By taking the lead on financial responsibility for her family, she developed a stronger sense of independence and a tough outer shell. Working from home, Mom did whatever it took to keep our family financially afloat, while also being present for Dad. To say she did it all is an understatement.

She took care of us, ran her own business, and worked various part-time jobs (some from home and some on the side). She was our personal chauffeur, shuttling us to school on the weekdays and Sunday school on the weekend so we could learn about our religion. Mom did not let fear drive her, and because she was curious about the possibility that she could be successful again, she thrived. Mom found happiness in Denver, and although it had taken a while, she finally accepted it as home, and she wouldn't dream of leaving.

Mom was passionate about rallying the local community of Afghans to address the need for more religious and cultural classes for Muslim children. Under her vision and guidance, the Afghan community bought a small building that they turned into a mosque/cultural center. Not only did she become the principal of the Sunday school, but she also taught all the children Dari and Islamic studies. Mom's accomplishments brought calm to the fears of many Afghan diaspora who felt they were losing their children to the American culture. Her passion to teach came from her previous days as an educator, and as she became the teacher and leader she had once been in Afghanistan, she was not only able to conquer her fears of moving to Denver, but she was also unintentionally squashing the female stereotype of Afghan Muslim women.

I saw how hard Mom worked, and although I could be an ungrateful teenager at times, I wasn't dense about the hurricane force she was. I respected her efforts and wanted to be a good daughter for her. I wanted to be the person she hoped I would be, someone strong and independent just like her. As I started to seek perfection in her eyes, I took life much more seriously and traded in my fun-loving personality for stability with my family. In doing so, I lost touch with the child that had once thrived on sunshine and beach water. She was a distraction to me. My focus was only to go to school, help take care of Dad, and cook and clean at home. Eventually, I became an extension of Mom's strong arm of support for our family.

Drama Queen

I didn't make many friends the rest of my school year in Colorado; I didn't really care to. I couldn't get close to anyone because sooner or later they would find out I wasn't a normal teenager that could come to their house or hang out at the movies with them on the weekends. Though my life appeared picture-perfect at home, I was struggling to fit in at school and continued to survive by shuffling my dual personalities.

My sophomore year of high school, I decided to give drama club a try. Somehow, I managed to land a leading role in the school play, *Arsenic and Old Lace*. Playing the part of Elaine, a distressed girlfriend, meant that I had to kiss a boy. This was a big step toward flat-out rebellion. I almost considered giving up the part, but the thought that I might be discovered by some famous agent who happened to be in the audience of a high school play in the middle of nowhere in Colorado was more intriguing, so I refused to turn it down. I was in teenage love with Keanu Reeves, and getting discovered was the only way he would ever notice me—a pimply, awkward 15-year-old. Besides, acting came naturally to me. I had already been playing multiple personality roles most of my life.

In a funny twist of events, Mom found out about the play from my brother and insisted on coming to see me. If that wasn't bad enough, she brought one of my male cousins along to join in on the fun. I was a nervous wreck, but I kept thinking about the famous agent that might be hanging out in the audience. *The show must go on!* As I entered the stage, the spotlight hit me, and I became Elaine. Right before I leaned in for the quick peck on the lips with my co-star, the whole audience went dead silent. You could hear a pin drop from the stage. In that moment, I heard a very distinct and familiar sigh come from the back of the audience. That quick peck was like a punch in the face to my mom, and I knew I had brought shame upon the house of Qudrat—but she wouldn't rat me out to my sick father though, would she?

The Consequences of Indecent Exposure

After the play, I was feeling very courageous for having moved forward with my decision. I begged my mom to let me go to the after party, and in a miraculous peer pressure driven moment with my drama teacher, she agreed. It was a dark and windy fall night, and as my ride home brought me closer and closer to the doorstep of my house, I felt a block of fear and regret lodge itself in my throat. What did Mom tell my dad? Was this going to change our relationship forever? How should I act? I hesitantly opened the door and walked in the house.

Dad was waiting for me in our dimly lit hallway with his hands crossed and his face fuming with anger. The narrow hallway of our home made him look more massive than he was. As he walked closer, I thought, *Oh shit! What have I done?* In one swift move, he came up behind me and half kicked, half pushed me from the front door into the house. Stumbling in, scared and surprised, I thought to myself, *How far is this going to go?* Dad stood in front of me in a very confrontational stance, raised his hand, and slapped me across the face.

Although he had not used the boxer force I knew he was capable of, he had never hit me before. This was new territory for all of us. With his eyes nearly bulging out of his head and his voice loud enough to wake the neighbors, he screamed at me for staying out late. In the midst of his thunderous rant, I was reminded of his deepest fears: that I was with people he didn't know and that they were probably 100 percent American. He continued to yell while I kept a stoic composure. I wanted him to be angry so I could justify my own anger.

When I entered the room my little sister was sharing with me, I could see the tears streaming from her glassy eyes. She didn't look up or make a sound, but I knew she was awake and had heard all the fighting. I climbed underneath the covers and finally broke down in tears. A feeling of guilt and sadness swept over me when I realized I had upset my sick father.

Stonewalling was my go-to reaction, so for the next few days, I avoided everyone by staying in my room. Awkward interactions with my dad in the mornings before school or in the evenings at the dinner table made it difficult to find the right time and place to give my elaborate half-assed apology. One afternoon, as I was returning home from school, I opened the door to find Dad sitting in the living room. I quickly said "hi" and continued heading toward my room, but before I could get very far, he intercepted my path. Wrapping his arms around my back, he pulled me close for a hug and apologized for his actions a few nights before. "Don't ever do that again," was all he said. That was all it took to open the floodgate of emotions for me, as I burst into tears in his arms.

Part of me was in shock because Afghan fathers didn't apologize to their unruly teenagers, yet here he was apologizing to me. Although I didn't realize it then, my stoic behavior since our altercation had scared my dad. He had never raised his hand to me before that night, and instead of crying on the floor asking for his forgiveness (as per his expectations), I stonewalled him. He knew I was capable of avoiding him for weeks at a time if I had to. Dad's plan to "set me straight" had backfired on him, and he quickly realized that I was more angry than apologetic for my behavior.

No parent wants that type of relationship with their children, especially my father. He had been a witness to how that had played out for other family members who had left their parents. So, instead of allowing this incident to bring division between us, Dad found a way to pull me closer and teach me the power of forgiveness. From that moment forward, I brushed away any feelings of anger or resentment, and I made a promise to never hurt or disobey him again. Nothing was worth losing my best friend in the most vulnerable moments of his life.

Lucky for my fearful parents, I was shaping up to be more like the person they saw in me: a girl who loved her parents and her family, and a girl who stayed close to her Afghan roots. My parents wanted to believe in my complete innocence, and I knew exactly what they needed to hear to make them feel safe and happy. Although Colorado was not the dark and isolated picture I had developed in my mind when we were first told we were moving there, an emotional transition had begun inside of me as I began to morph into someone other than who I really was.

16

From Goth to Hijab

I didn't hang around the cool kids at school, but that didn't matter to me. Of course I wanted friends, but I found more comfort in being home, where I didn't have to explain myself to anyone. I had one real friend throughout high school who was from India and she had strict parents like me. We conversed about living as "brown people" and found comfort in knowing that weird and confused people like us existed. Once, in our objective to prove that we were independent and rebellious teenagers, we were able to convince our parents to let us go to dinner together. Instead of eating out, we actually snuck out to crash a school dance for a few hours, but no one had to know that. The rebellion manifested in many other ways. A couple times I was able to leave Colorado and visit my cousins in California without my family. To my parents' unbeknownst eyes and ears, my cousins and I would sneak out to fancy nightclubs in Hollywood. Fake IDs and lots of makeup turned us into "normal" rebellious American girls for a night or two before returning to our harsh reality. My parents had zero view of this; however, the anger of living perfectly would sometimes rise to the surface. Upon my return to Colorado, I would remember how different my life could have been in California and my emotional uproar increased.

I disliked that people (mostly high schoolers) in Colorado were either ignorant about where Afghanistan was or had zero knowledge of world events. For all anyone was concerned, I was from some desert country in the Middle East, a place known for war and gasoline. I was sick of looking different, and at one point I wished that I could just be a "normal" white person and say that I was from some small town in the middle of Ohio. Nothing became more appealing to me than to blend into the crowd.

On one dark and dreary day, (okay, I don't remember if it was dark and dreary or not, but go with me on this) I decided that I was a *goth*. Subscribing to the bare minimum requirements of being considered goth, I blasted The Cure on the radio, wore black lipstick, and turned the knobs on my hormone dispenser to depressed and angry. Suddenly, I found it was easier to accept all the change that was happening in my life. It was pure rebellion, and it allowed me to feel like I had some semblance of control over my look. It also made it easier not to have friends, because when you are goth, loner behavior is expected and even cool. Those that I called my friends were actually just acquaintances, but that was just fine with me.

I would, however, remove my black lipstick before Mom or Dad would pick me up from school. They could not know that my fashion choices were a combination of black over black or that my inspiration was Trent Reznor from the band Nine Inch Nails. My parents were not in their graves yet, and I didn't want to prematurely put them there.

Adventures with P.J.

Turning 16 granted me the ultimate source of freedom: driving. I bought my first car, a white Jeep Wrangler, and paid for it by working as a telemarketer and receptionist at my dad's small cartridge recycling business. Yes, he continued to be a hard-working hustler even while he was fighting cancer.

P.J. was my car's name, and she was my favorite possession in the world. I drove her all over the place. She took me to every hiking spot in the nearby foothills, and if I could get the opportunity to take a 30-minute adventure on my way to the library or take the long way home after picking up milk from the grocery store, I embraced it. Even today, I love to just get on the road and drive to a spontaneous location.

My husband recently asked me, "What in this world makes you feel like a rich person?"

I answered, "A full tank of gas."

To me, my car was a symbol of ultimate freedom. Whenever I was inside, I could be myself and reflect on life or blast whatever music I wanted.

Having a car took me to the mountains and ski resorts of Colorado, and I fell in love with snowboarding. I took every opportunity to go to the mountains just so I could watch other seasoned snowboarders perform fancy tricks and flips down the slopes. I wasn't great at it myself, especially in the beginning, but with every trip to the bunny slopes, I got better at maintaining my balance and learning how to fall correctly.

We weren't rich, so we didn't enroll in the expensive classes that offered expert advice or one-on-ones. If we had extra money, we would buy ski lift tickets; if not, we just hung out at the bunny slopes and went up and down a hundred times. My family stood out because we were typically the only brown people on the mountains. We wore our jeans and chunky sweaters instead of proper ski gear on the slopes, which often caught the eye of the more affluent white population that scurried around us. Uncommon outfits and loud laughter from our group sometimes made us the center of attention. I ignored the uncomfortable stares of others and stay determined enough to teach myself all the basics of snowboarding. While the ski gear and lessons certainly aide in a better experience, I found that the only requirement to the sport is that you cannot give up, no matter how hard you fall or how uncomfortable it becomes to stand out. Not only is that good advice for any athlete, but it is also a great mantra for life.

College Dreams

I wasn't a 4.0 student in high school, but I was a good student who finally learned how to behave in class. My teachers often commented on my potential to "do great things" in the future, and it was through their support I gained confidence in my ability to succeed academically. My parents wanted me to be a doctor, but I wasn't thrilled with the idea of dealing with blood and guts. In true Shahira fashion, journalism and law claimed the top spots on my list of passions. Though I had ambitions I knew I could never realistically plan for, I did not stop dreaming about becoming the next Christiane Amanpour or Barbara Walters.

I wanted to travel the world by myself and even go to some prestigious school in England; however, I knew that my parents wouldn't allow me to live anywhere but home. They cared too much about traditional Afghan norms, and Dad did not want to be considered to be another Afghan-American who was losing his cultural identity like the rest.

At 17, I graduated a semester early and ready to take a break before I entered higher education. In my senior year I was offered a full ride scholarship to the University of Colorado Boulder. (Yes, you read that correctly—four years of college for *free!*) It was the perfect choice of school for my ambitions and only 30 minutes away from home. Unfortunately, the dorm requirements were non-negotiable for all recipients of the scholarship, and my parent's had to sign on the dotted line that would take me out of my home and into a small dorm to be shared with a stranger. I could picture what was running through my parents' brains as they informed me of their decision not to let me attend: me chugging beer with a group of boys in the middle of some frat shindig, like in the 1984 movie *Party Animal.* Upon hearing the news, I silently walked away from my parents and sat inside P.J., crying for hours in my driveway. The nightmare of a college rebellion was too powerful for my parents to give any ground on this issue.

According to my parents, it was not acceptable for good, single Afghan girls to leave their homes before marriage, and school was no exception. What was even more unfortunate was that by this time in my life, I had stopped asking "Why?" I understood the cultural sensitivities, and was too paralyzed by the fear of breaking away from my family to pursue my career ambitions from afar so I stayed close to home to make my parents happy—especially my dad. His health was declining, and I was becoming second in line as his caregiver. We settled on a nearby community college. While it wasn't my first, second, or third pick for school, it was better than no school at all.

Like his health, Dad's small business began dwindling. We condensed the toner cartridge recycling business into the garage, and my father started driving a taxi cab instead. I happily took a part-time job in a corporate office mailroom to make sure P.J. and I had fuel for future adventures. The combination of school and a new job made my life fun and exciting for once, and I did not have to hide it! I was at the precipice of authentic self-discovery, though still looking out at the world with the safety goggles my parents had provided me.

Spending Time with God

Being in college gave me the space to explore spirituality. I wanted to know more about God and how people around the world demonstrated devotion to their creator(s). Fantasies about walking inside the Sistine Chapel filled my head, as I dreamed about *The Last Judgment*, Michelangelo's passionate painting devoted to God. I envisioned myself climbing the Mayan Pyramid of the Sun in Mexico, and standing in the same place as the ancient Aztec leaders. I imagined myself in Mecca, performing the Muslim pilgrimage and sleeping outside under the same stars the Prophet Muhammad did. It did not matter what religion I was studying because they were all acts of devotion manifesting in amazing ways.

I became curious about how people turned to God in times of need or how they viewed God in their times of challenge. Through my studies, I found many similarities between Islam, Christianity, and Judaism, which made me begin to see people in a different light. If people of differing religions could connect on the common ground of simply being human beings, maybe they would find the key to true brotherhood.

Our little library at home was stocked with hundreds of books about Islam that my mom had collected over the years as a Sunday school teacher. Blowing the dust from some of the books, I read them again from a totally new perspective. I was no longer a rebellious teenager forced to wake up early on a Sunday morning and drive 45 minutes to get to the local mosque to pray because my parents made me. I was now 18, and it was my responsibility to learn what I was supposed to believe as a Muslim and either affirm the faith that my parents had passed onto me or bring to the surface any doubts.

I was finally taking a stance in one area of my life. Being more conscious of God brought me a sense of inner peace and like my mom, I dedicated Sundays to teaching younger kids about Islam. I knew that by teaching others, I could learn more about how God enters lives. Aside from that, being around children gave me joy, especially when my students asked really difficult questions that would take me a week to ponder and research.

I started following what I believed to be the rulebook of Islam, religiously engaging in the prescriptive prayers five times a day. While I had prayed throughout my teenage years, I had never made a commitment to pray in the marathon fashion required in the Islamic faith. Forcing myself to sit down to meditate and reflect on my day went against my passive nature, but it made me work hard to build new habits. No matter what religion you subscribe to, praying five times a day will make you a more conscious human being. Praying gave me a direct link to God, which allowed me to start to have very honest conversations with my Creator. I didn't realize it then, but the perseverance of my curiosity and the conversations I had with God about life would get me through some really rough times later.

My weekend and evening plans were atypical for a girl my age. While others went out to party or go to the movies with friends, I stayed home reading the Quran (the holy book of Muslims, sometimes spelled as Koran). The process was tedious and took a lot of time, considering I read Arabic at a first grade level and had to research hundreds of other books in English about specific meanings. The volumes and volumes of translations in our library formed a wall on my desk, and the task to read them to completion became daunting. I badly wanted to understand the Quran's meaning, but this practice became difficult to keep up with, and I wasn't making any progress. So, I chose to motivate myself by memorizing the Arabic text first with the intention of researching the meaning later. In hindsight, I had settled in the *Comfort Zone*, which caused me to rush the learning process and stop asking the most important question—why?

One day, while I was leaving the Muslim Student Association office after prayer, I hastily decided not to remove the scarf wrapped around my hair. The scarf (also called a hijab) is worn by Muslim women to demonstrate modesty and devotion to God. Previously, I had only covered my hair in the presence of God as a requirement for prayer; however, something inside me nudged me to keep it on that day. For the most part, I figured it would give me the experience of understanding how it feels to wear a hijab in public, then I could take it off later before I went to work. Surprisingly, having strangers stare at me didn't make me feel uncomfortable or nervous like I thought it would. Perhaps it was because my social circle mostly consisted of women who also wore hijabs, or maybe it was because I didn't mind becoming anonymous. Whatever it was, from that day on, I decided to roll with it and continue covering my hair.

Ironically, Dad wasn't a fan of my scarf. One day, as I was walking out the door to go to school, he stopped me and said, "Can you stop looking so Arab when you leave the house?"

I stopped dead in my tracks, took a deep breath, quickly rolled my eyes before he could see, and then turned around to face him. "*Padar* [which means father in Dari], I am wearing the hijab for myself. It has nothing to do with Arabs!"

He asked me if I could at least tone down the "Arab look" by wearing the Afghan version of the scarf, which is a less obvious transparent fabric. He was not fond of Arabs or Arab politics, so I knew where the concern was coming from.

It took some guts, but I stood my ground. "*Padar*, I don't like the Afghan hijab. It doesn't even cover my hair. What is the point?"

I wasn't going to water down my interpretation of modesty, and for the first time, I walked away the victor in a debate with Dad. He stood in the driveway as I got into my car. Knowing he was annoyed with me, I loosened up my scarf by tying it around my neck Persian/Iranian style to make him a little more comfortable. He smiled and waved at me as I backed out of the driveway. *Crap! Did I just lose the debate again?* After that, he never commented on my head scarf again, but probably because he was afraid to drive me into rebelling by wearing a short skirt and tank top instead.

The truth is, I didn't care what type of fabric was on my head. It's never about the look, quality, or texture of the 24 inches by 48 inches piece of fabric, but it's about the tangible symbol of my devotion to God. It was liberating to free myself from the opinion of others. Wearing the hijab was *my* choice, and I was proud to be able to express my faith outwardly. I had no idea there would be so much controversy around the topic in the coming years of American history.

The scarf had become my solace and sanctuary from the outside world. I didn't have to wear makeup, get dressed, or do my hair to impress anyone. Of course, I did those things for myself when I wanted to, but I ultimately found pleasure in living my life free of society's irrational expectations. When I was wearing the scarf for the right reasons, I didn't feel oppressed. In fact, I felt quite the opposite. That's right! I felt more freedom. The act of freeing oneself from the *dunya* (Dari word for the material world) was new territory for me, because I had been so attached to family and what people thought of me. There are few times in my life that I have felt completely at peace. Finding my way to God and expressing it outwardly by detaching from this world was one of those times.

Although my head covering had given me a new sense of identity as a Muslim, I still wasn't sure what I wanted to be when I grew up. All the adventurous endeavors I had pictured in my head were starting to become less and less possible in my eyes. Even though I didn't have an exact path laid out in front of me or a specific career in mind, I kept my options open. New subjects every semester were enough to satisfy my curiosity until I could pinpoint my future profession.

I spent hours at the library studying for exams, and only left when I had to go to work or just before sundown, when it was time to head home. While this may seem simplistic, I was happy to have something that was *just* for me. I was allowing myself to be free and independent. Even better than that, it made me a "good girl" in the eyes of my family, and my parents were pleased with me. I thought I had it all figured out.

Looking Back

With a physical symbol of my devotion wrapped around my head and an increasing understanding of Islamic traditions inside my head, I became arrogant and judgmental of women and men who did not follow the religion as I had interpreted it. Most of it was subconscious, but I was developing an "us" and "them" mentality. *That poor lost soul*, I would think as a young Muslim woman without a scarf would walk by me. Various texts I had read had rigid interpretations of Islam, and as a result, my views were changing, and not for the better.

In my immaturity, I began excluding others who did not look like me. I started going against the tenants of my own faith in order to play the part I thought the world wanted me to play. Instead of praying five times a day to continue my conversations with God, I was praying in robot fashion, only keeping track of how many "*rakahs*" or completed rituals I prayed. Most importantly, I stopped asking "why" I was following these different traditions, and I started to take in each verse at face value.

No one was responsible for my wretched interpretation for Islam except for me. I thought I was being a good Muslim, but I embodied neither the true meaning of Islam nor the concept of inclusivity. Unfortunately, my actions were taking me further away from the inner peace and solace I had been searching for. It would be years before I made my peace with God again.

The Fading Warrior

With the passing of each day, Dad's body would age as though years had gone by. When we were living in California, he was over six feet tall and weighed 250 pounds, but his illness had given him a new face, one with hollow eyes and pale skin. Helplessly, I watched as his massive body became paper thin right before my eyes. He would often skip visits to the doctor, as he would become more bitter and heartbroken every time the doctors informed him that they could not improve the quality of his life.

After one of Dad's surgeries, a colostomy bag was attached to his lower abdomen. The doctors had cut his colon in half and attached it to the outer wall of his abdomen with a small bag attached to his body to collect waste. Though the medical procedure had sent the Grim Reaper away for a few more years, Dad had changed, often grieving the loss of his physical identity. Because his health left him unable to drive his taxi for more than a few hours a day, he was no longer the traditional breadwinner in our family. While Dad was supportive of Mom stepping in to financially support us, I cannot imagine what a blow it was to his ego and identity as the man of the family.

Addictions

The drastic rate of change in his health coupled with his inability to control his bodily functions really affected Dad's personality. Chemotherapy left him in extreme pain, and the huge appetite he used to have for Mom's home cooking was no more. He started seeing doctors who specialized in pain management instead of the surgeons who would inform him that his cancer was spreading like wildfire. The pain management specialists prescribed him many controlled medications, though I would argue that they were *not* well controlled. The medications, especially the morphine, took the pain away at first, but over time its potency became limited. When one pill wasn't enough, he took two or sometimes three at a time.

Gradually, the doctors prescribed him more and more drugs until his days were full of brainless slumber. One of his doctors said to me, "Pain is like a sponge. You just keep adding medication until the sponge is soaked up and the pain goes away." Again, I am not a doctor, but I am not convinced that this statement is true, especially in my dad's case. I believe Dad became a morphine and OxyContin addict because the doctors kept adding to his dosage.

Although my youngest brother was the apple of my dad's eye, he and my dad weren't able to interact much after we moved to Colorado. On top of that, he could no longer play or be his loud, six-year-old, rambunctious self because when Dad was sleeping, any disturbance meant he would wake up screaming in agony. So, instead of play fighting or boxing with Dad like my other siblings and I used to, my brother was often sent to his room where he was set up with video games to keep him busy. Sitting in front of the TV for hours, he missed the opportunity to have a relationship with my parents, and as a result, my little brother grew up with a dependence on technology; and we allowed it to happen. It was just easier to move him to the side and focus on tending to Dad and his needs.

Even though Dad was extremely ill, he would occasionally have a good day, which for him meant less pain. Our family would pile into his favorite car—a classic Blue Toyota Land Cruiser that we customized by adding an old mattress in the cargo space for him. Taking the lead, I would drive us into the mountains where he could be at peace for a short time. We spent many hours together as a family in that car singing stupid songs or commenting about how the sky looked endless as we drove further and further from civilization. After a two-hour drive, we would arrive at his favorite place—a place he called *Sari Zameen* (Dari for the phrase "on our land"). Sari Zameen is a small plot of land my father bought in a small mountainside resort when we first moved to Colorado. It looked a lot like the painting of Colorado I had created in my head when I was 14. Upon arrival, we would setup our picnic spot, and walk him over near the creek that runs through the land. And just like old times, Mom would set up a picnic area where we could be loud and boisterous again, even if it was for a short time. My family still owns this piece of land, and although we haven't built Dad's dream cabin yet, our intention is to do so one day, so we can relive some of the wonderful memories with our own children.

Grind Through the Pain

My family and I grieved for a long period of time. We knew it was only a matter of time before death showed up at our door, but we did not know how to prepare for the hurt and pain it would cause. Because of the stigma around mental health in our culture, it was only "crazy people" who saw counselors or therapists, so we didn't believe we needed anyone to help us get through this difficult time in our lives. We did what we had to do in order to survive the difficult moments, but it was taking an emotional toll on my whole family.

Dad's illness meant that my brothers lost their mentor and teacher in life. Any guidance he could have provided was no longer available to them, because the combination of the pain pills and the daily grind made it impossible. My younger sister was helping around the house more often, but she mainly focused on her schoolwork to distract her from the pain. She was the academic star in the family, so my parents wanted her to focus on studying to fulfill her dreams of being a doctor. Her heart was breaking, but because she was so young, no one could see the pieces.

Instead of talking about how we were being impacted, we all found ways to keep busy, hoping one day we would wake up from this nightmare. Emotional instability had its fingers wrapped around all of us, but pride and the fear of dealing with our problems in an authentic and honest manner kept us from loosening its grasp. We had to be strong for Dad, but even more so for Mom, who was busy working 16-hour days to provide for us.

They say that hardships create opportunities for teenagers to build character, but what happens when a teenager is emotionally immature and questioning her basic identity? I rarely cried or showed emotion at home because I wanted everyone to know that I wouldn't lose my shit if anything happened. Putting on a façade was my specialty, so you would never see tears roll down my face in public (that was what P.J. was for). My dad, our warrior, was fading, and I was about to face some of the biggest decisions of my life.

18

A Premature Fall into Womanhood

When I was a senior in high school, my family had some un-expected visitors. "We have come to ask you for your daughter's hand in marriage to our son," they stated. There was only one problem: I had no idea who their son was or what he looked like, and neither did my parents. While the offer was both flattering and confusing, I told my parents that since I was just about to start college, I was not interested. Dad was happy with my decision to pass on the offer, because he did not know the family and he was hesitant about accepting proposals from families he didn't know. It was easy for me to tell him no when I already knew that was what he wanted to hear.

After this happened a few more times, the situation was be-coming all too real. I was growing up, and for a good Afghan girl, it's not love that comes first, it's marriage. Not long after I began attending college, my extended family on Mom's side proposed that I marry my cousin Shabir, who had recently moved from India to America. Receiving so many marriage proposals from other families had made my extended family think I was at risk for being "lost" to another family, so they jumped on the "Niggin bandwagon" before I could say yes to someone else.

Since Shabir and I had grown up on opposite sides of the globe, he was a complete stranger in my eyes. He spoke very refined Dari and dressed in golf shirts and slacks instead of the all black suits and leather jackets that I was drawn to. Naturally, I wasn't attracted to him, but that was firstly because he was my cousin, and secondly, because we didn't have much in common. In fact, I was a bit appalled at my family's suggestion, but when I mentioned my shock to both Mom and Dad, they did not jibe with my feelings. Instead, they lectured me about being an Afghan girl, often reminding me that marrying into the family was honorable. Dad furthered the discussion by telling the story of his arranged marriage to Mom and how they had grown to be as happy as clams.

Dad was right—family arranged marriages were, and continue to be, normal occurrences in Southeast Asia and the Middle East, but we weren't in the Middle East. We were in America! Nonetheless, the counter debate of being against family arranged marriages wasn't a winning argument with my parents, because half of the Afghan community that we socialized with in Colorado were married to their cousins. Some couples had kids while others didn't, and some seemed happy in their arranged marriages, while others appeared miserable. The hard truth I had to swallow was that the tradition of family arranged marriage is as much alive today as it was thousands of years ago, and it was my turn to jump in the hot seat.

A few days after I had received the initial lecture from my parents, Dad sat me down to talk about it again. With my cheeks flushing red, I sat down. I had never talked to my dad about guys, marriage, or relationships prior to this situation. "You are an Afghan girl," he reiterated, "and this is an honorable thing for you to do." To him, marriage proposals meant that he and my mom had raised a good Afghan girl with a good reputation. Unfortunately for me, I was at a fork in the road of my life, and I was not sure how to reply to my parents.

As the conversation continued with Dad, I did not say much. I was attempting to understand why he was so supportive of this engagement and not the proposals from other families. It became crystal clear, when these words came out of his mouth: "Before I die, I want to see you taken care of." The words are etched in my brain forever, because I realized that I was willing to do anything to make him happy, even if it meant doing something that didn't make me happy.

Dad was dying, and we all knew his time was close. I knew that by accepting this proposal, I would be helping my dad experience some sense of peace in the inevitably short years ahead of him. So, I was going to fulfill my *good girl prophecy* by doing exactly what he wanted. Hesitantly, I nodded and said, "Okay." The room was silent for a few moments before anyone spoke. Mom was also in the room but had kept quiet, playing more of an observer role. Later, she told me that she was thinking that if anything went south in the relationship, she would have to deal with the brunt of it. Mom was not against the engagement, but she wasn't supportive of it either. After all, it was her sister's son, and what an awkward situation for her to be involved in if she had to pick sides one day!

Mom asked me, "Are you sure?" I just sat there numb, nodding my head as I stared at the aging hands of my dad. He was too young to look as frail as he did, and a feeling of sadness rushed over me. He took the next few moments of silence as final consent and then asked Mom to call my aunt and let her know the good news. I remember thinking to myself, *How the hell could this happen? Why don't I stop him? If this is good news, why don't I feel good? Why am I going through this moral dilemma at such a young age?* My siblings had no idea what was happening, so they were shocked when they found out that the news wasn't a joke.

Although I had started developing relationships with other Afghan girls in college, I had no real close friends in whom to confide. Even if I did, would they really understand my situation? I kept asking God for a way out, however, my approach was self-victimizing, a coping mechanism to justify the decision I had made. You know, something like, "Poor me. I *had* to do this for my dad." There would be moments that I would accept it and swallow whatever emotions came with it, but there were other times where I would think, *This isn't happening! Somebody yell, 'Cut!' so we can end this scene and rewind to three years ago!* I was an emotional wreck and battling feelings of denial and anger. As difficult as it was, the battles were only happening in my head, so no one could see the raging soldiers of morality dying behind my fake smile. It was only P.J. who could attest to the tears and sorrow I felt.

"You're not getting cold fins now, are you?"

~ *The Little Mermaid*

P.J. spent the next few days with me in the driveway, providing a safe space for me to cry. I spent a lot of time pondering how this decision was going to define me. Something didn't feel right inside of me. I was in the United States; not some far away third-world country where stuff like this was normal. I used to laugh and joke with my school friends about the stereotypical hillbillies in Kentucky who would partake in incestual behavior, and now I would be entering into a similar situation. I told myself that I would not let anyone know that he was my cousin. If anyone asked, I could just say that he was a close family friend. I lied to all of my co-workers and friends because they would never understand. I lied to everyone, including myself.

A week later, I was sitting in a car in the parking lot of my aunt's apartment building. I had driven there with my mom, but I didn't want to go inside. I needed more time to compose myself and accept the decision I had made as final, so I stayed in the car while Mom ran up the stairs to my aunt's apartment.

Alone in the car, I fell apart. Thinking no one could see or hear me under my scarf, I burst into tears. While I had been sobbing into my tear drenched hands, my Uncle Max had driven up and parked next to me. I had been so consumed with crying that I didn't hear him until his large hands started tapping on my car window. Once I rolled the window down, he stuck his head in the car. I quickly wiped my tears and tried to suck the snot back into my nose. Maybe if I smiled he wouldn't notice the tears or my swollen red eyes.

Uncle Max kissed my wet cheek before a look of concern flashed across his face. "If anyone is forcing you to say yes, tell me now, and I will set them straight," he said, giving me the same mob boss look he had given me back when he had forced the five-dollar bill into my hands. This time, however, the cultural crime I wanted to commit involved not only myself, but Dad's word and reputation as well.

I was so emotional that I started bawling and shaking my head against the hot vinyl of the driving wheel. "No, no, no," I repeated over and over again. How could I explain the emotions I was feeling? How could I tell him that though I didn't want this for myself, I had decided to do it to make Dad happy? What would my dad do if I ended the façade here? If cancer didn't kill him, maybe the dishonorable decision I wanted to make would. Even though I was screaming inside my head, all the words got caught in my throat. After a minute of holding my head in my hands, I looked up and told him that everything was fine and that I was just crying because I was thinking of Dad and how sick he was. I wasn't lying. I was sad and thinking of nobody else but Dad.

Looking back now, I realize that this moment was a very defining point in my life. In a perfect world, I would have told my Uncle Max exactly how I felt. Would it have caused a commotion? Yes. Would it have upset my family if I had taken my decision back? Yes. Would it have been more authentic of me to tell Dad and Mom how I really felt and stood my ground? Yes. They say hindsight is 20/20, and in this case, I wish I could transport myself back to this moment and say the things I wish I would have said instead of staying silent.

While I do not dwell on the past, my observations and the lessons learned along the way are most important to the unfurling of this story. Trust between parents and children can be cultivated, and while it might be difficult to deal with a seemingly defiant child in the moment, it is not the end of the world to be on the opposite side of the fence on issues that define values or principles. There is beauty in diversity among humans, even in the form of varying value systems within the family structure.

I Think I Do

While my family spent all their money planning a lavish engagement party for the Afghan community, I made a decision that I wasn't going to share my true emotions with anyone. Since no one was going to understand my perspective anyway, I kept my mouth shut and continued down the path I had started paving for myself. I made a choice to remove the victim mentality and focus on the positive. Through this marriage I would gain an honorable mode of independence from my parents and the opportunity to be on my own. I could finally have a place of my own, continue to go to school and work if I wanted to, and maybe even travel if I wanted to.

But let's not forget the fact that I was only 18 years old and would have to spend the bulk of my time with someone I barely knew. Yes, he was family, and yes I knew of him, but that didn't matter. It was as if I was in Mom's shoes when her hand in marriage was promised to Dad. I kept telling myself, "You are an Afghan woman, and this is completely normal." I said it enough times that I made myself believe it, and wiped out any American identifiers that came with it.

As a mother of a teenager now, I often think, *What the heck does an 18-year-old know about life, let alone marriage?* I was on a fast track to adulthood, and while I could argue that I was responsible for my age, I had never experienced an intimate relationship with another person. I always thought I would fall in love with a prince charming type, like Ariel did with Prince Eric. I imagined my prince charming would tell his parents, I would tell mine, our families would meet, and then I would turn into a mermaid and live a normal American life. Remember the tune we used to sing in elementary school? "First comes love, then comes marriage, then comes the baby in the baby carriage." Someone must have accidentally transposed the first two nouns of that song in Afghanistan, right?

While I wasn't looking for a fairytale (or maybe I was), I was hoping that my marriage would at least be based on what I understood to be "love." Since I couldn't have that, I would have to try to find something else to base my relationship on. Instead of love, I chose respect. If I could somehow find respect for Shabir, maybe this whole situation would turn out better than expected.

The engagement and wedding ceremonies were a blur. Very few of the details are vivid in my mind. There are even pictures I am in that I don't remember taking. In the Afghan culture, the bride's family plans, coordinates, and pays for the engagement party. It is an event worthy of honor, and my parents were proud to be hosting it. Of course they were financially struggling, but that was not going to stop them.

Although Dad was really sick, he drove his taxi for long hours once again. Mom, who was going to school to complete her associate's degree in business, didn't sleep for three months. She worked crazy hours at her own gas station business and processed medical bills from home in the evening. My parents worked extra hours and used all the money they were saving to pay for the engagement party. They even flew in a master chef from California and an Afghan singer and his band from another city to be at the event.

The party was a hit. More than 500 people attended, but I didn't know two-thirds of them. They were all acquaintances of my parents, and most of them knew Mom from her religious and cultural involvement in the Afghan community. For me it was like being in the shoes of a politician, hugging and greeting everyone, kissing babies, and shaking the hands of people I didn't know.

I spent the next few months before marriage getting to know Shabir. He was a religious man and spent a lot of time in the mosque. I assume he liked me because I looked very Muslim with my headscarf, I stayed quiet, and I was not a very high maintenance gal at all. It was my maternal grandmother's dream for us to be married, and because she had been a big influence on his life, he felt that he was honoring her wishes, since she had passed on a few years earlier.

Shabir looked like the typical Muslim man with brown skin, dark eyes, a beard, and traditional Islamic clothing, which he wore often. His religious views were similar to what I was practicing, and we found common ground in practicing our faith together. We were becoming amicable friends, and I tried very hard to see the world from his perspective. His mannerisms were strange, and because he hadn't been raised with any American values, I often struggled to explain my perspective. When I knew I wasn't making any progress, I just stopped talking altogether.

Shabir and I spent a lot of time watching Hollywood and Bollywood movies, because it was easier just to stare at a screen together. Respecting him was all that was necessary in my eyes to make the relationship work. No one had to know my feelings on the inside. That was between me and God, and God was hearing an earful from me during that season of my life.

I Did

Against the wishes of my parents, we had a small wedding at the local mosque where Mom had been heavily involved. This angered my parents, especially Dad, because the engagement party had been so big and extravagant. Somehow, Shabir managed to respectfully convince Dad that a small wedding was a good idea. As for me, I had no opinion. I was just playing along. I was more passionate about picking out my first set of couches than planning any wedding, big or small.

Over time I found less and less in common with Shabir, so I happily invited any distraction that didn't have anything to do with us working on our relationship. I was lucky in that Shabir was a non-confrontational person and didn't want to talk about any difficult subjects, such as how I really felt about the marriage or what I really wanted to do with my life. My passive behaviors, as well as his, made it a seemingly peaceful relationship. But if we had spoken honestly, there wouldn't be a relationship.

Given the variety of doubtful feelings I had circling in my brain about the choices I had made, I turned to anything that could keep me busy. Avoidance behaviors, such as staying at my parents' house all the time or not speaking up when I didn't agree with my husband, caused me to bury my true emotions deep inside my heart. I thought to myself, *I should have a child*, because then I could have someone to love unconditionally, and I wouldn't have to work on my relationship problems.

While I accepted that I had married into the family, I didn't want to risk having kids that would have genetic problems (like those Kentucky kids did). After a lot of research, I was fortunate to find a Chinese doctor who understood my cultural dilemma. She was familiar with family arranged marriages and even marriage within families, because it was prevalent in her culture as well. She performed a genetic panel test and assured me that the chances of genetic problems in our children were very low. Once we were cleared, I decided that the next natural step after being married was to have children, just like the elementary song said.

Unfortunately, in the world of a 19-year-old, a big decision like having a baby can be justified for many reasons; even reasons that aren't sensible or logical. I didn't understand the sheer responsibility of having a child. I just knew that I was good with children, and I wanted to love and feel loved. I had practically raised my siblings, so that qualified me to be a parent, right?

9/11

They say that everyone remembers where they were when they first heard about the events of 9/11. I certainly do. It was my eighth month of pregnancy, and I was in the doctor's office for an early morning prenatal visit. As I entered the office, there was a strange feeling in the air, perhaps because of how unusually quiet the place was. On my way to the exam room, all of the familiar faces of nurses who were usually running around the office were crowded around a small television in the break room. Briefly, I caught a glimpse of a Muslim-looking man and a burning building in the background.

"Hey, Alice. What's happening in there?" I asked curiously, when my nurse came to check my vitals.

"New York is under a terrorist attack, and hundreds of people are dead," she replied, her voice trembling.

Before she could finish her sentence, I could feel my heart sink to the bottom of my feet. "Please don't be Muslim," I whispered repeatedly to myself.

When Alice checked my blood pressure, she noticed it was high and asked me if I was feeling okay. There I was, visibly Muslim, extremely pregnant, and scared as hell about what was happening in the world.

No! I am not okay! I thought to myself. If that guy I had seen on the TV was a Muslim, and if he had truly caused all that death and destruction, women like me who wore headscarves and men who looked like him were about to enter a season of violent storms. The large group of people around the world who called themselves Muslims were going to pay the price for the actions of a small group of extremist individuals. Unfortunately, I was right.

The Toll of 9/11

Attitudes toward Muslims turned negative overnight, and the term "terrorist" became the label for thousands of people all over the world. Islam became a disease the media wanted to treat, and consequently, hate crimes against Muslims increased at tremendous rates, causing an identity crisis for many American Muslims. Because women who were visibly Muslim were viewed as an ominous representation of this mysterious and perceptually barbaric religion, many women stayed home, so as not to put themselves or their children at risk. A simple rectangular piece of fabric that was supposed to be a symbol of devotion to God had become a symbol of hate, oppression, and death.

After the events of 9/11, Muslim people had to take a step back and dig deep about their beliefs—at least I know I did. I feared speaking authentically, because I knew we were living under a microscope, with our lives and privacy subject to open monitoring and public scrutiny. I would find myself over-apologizing for the loss of life on 9/11, as if I was the one who committed the crime. When verses from the Quran were taken out of context, people like me were forced to defend historical events and explain Arabic linguistics. No Muslim could really be himself or herself, because we had to censor our perspective for fear of misinterpretation or persecution. While the reputation of Muslims in America has come a long way since 9/11, there is still a lot of hate against Muslims, mostly rooted in subconscious ignorance.

The events of 9/11 seemed to have had a very deep impact on Shabir; deeper than I could understand at the time. Though we generally didn't speak to each other at home, after the attack happened he became very anxious and started talking more— mostly about conspiracy theories in relation to the events of 9/11. His appetite changed, and he started staying awake for days at a time, either working or blasting extremely loud music in our small apartment.

To make matters more complicated, one day he would be spewing ideas of grandeur and talking about how we were on our way to becoming millionaires because he had a business idea that could not fail, and the next week he would stay in bed for days, refusing to get up and face the world as it was for Muslims. I usually just laughed at his quirky behavior, chalking it up to our cultural differences, but what I didn't realize is that there was a storm brewing.

Because of Shabir's strong religious ties in the community, the FBI paid my family many visits. When his paranoia and bi-polar disorder symptoms kicked in, Shabir would say things like "People are watching us," or "God will punish the offenders," and it would make him and our family a bigger target for questioning by the authorities. Out of fear, he and his friends purchased rifles to "protect" their families. Shabir placed the rifles under the mattress, right under my side of the bed, just in case someone tried to attack us in the middle of the night. The FBI documented the serial numbers from the guns and continued to come to our house weekly.

To someone looking in from the outside, Shabir's behavior was very suspicious. As an American, I understood that. The FBI had come to our house so many times that I had started calling the agents by their first names and knew if they took their coffee with cream or sugar. They questioned me about Shabir's comments and behaviors, and all I could do was shake my head and assure them that we were not terrorists, but two people reacting in fear in order to protect ourselves. After a few months of digging around, the FBI was unable to find anything incriminating, and they realized that Shabir was suffering from a mental illness, so their visits came to a halt. Our phones were still tapped long after their visits, but I didn't care. I had nothing to hide!

Express Lane: English Speakers Only, Please

Whenever I was in public, I never experienced any physical violence, but people were generally rude to me, and some were even hostile. One afternoon, while in line at a grocery store with Mom, someone tapped my shoulder and asked, "Hey, do you even know how speak or read English?" While the question itself wasn't necessarily rude, the eyes of the woman who was asking told a different story. Out of shock, I didn't respond right away. Instead, I took a step back to mentally assess what had just happened. The elderly white woman continued to scowl at me, but I was confused about why. Then she moved into my personal bubble, coming so close to my face that I could feel the heat from her red flushed cheeks. "Can't you read the sign?" she asked, pointing to the bright cashier light that indicated we were in lane number four.

Apparently, Mom and I were standing in the "express lane" of the supermarket without realizing it, and our basket had more than the 15 allowed items. I quickly gathered my thoughts and responded to the woman. "I am sorry. My mother and I made a mistake. We will move to lane number five, but why are you making the assumption that I do not speak English?"

The woman was taken aback by my American accent. Clearly, that was not what she was expecting. She backed her grocery cart away from us and proceeded into the store, but not before hurling one more insult. "God damn Muslim foreigners. Go back to your country, you damn terrorists!" I called her a racist and told her I would call the police if she approached me again.

Others around us stayed silent, but it was evident that they were mostly relieved that the situation had diffused the way it did. While I ended up reporting the incident to the grocery store manager, I wasn't sure what he could do. He apologized for the woman's behavior and stated that if she would have become physical with us, he would have called the police. I am not sure I believed him.

Personally, I felt like it was my duty to continue wearing the headscarf after 9/11. The glares that had gone unnoticed in the past were now like laser beams burning small holes through my body, but I kept telling myself that my purpose in such moments was to demonstrate the real face of Islam which lived in me and others who were peaceful at heart. Wearing my headscarf in the community was a challenge, but I found purpose in the act of being Muslim American in a time where ignorance was prevalent.

Continuing to take school classes helped me cope with the tough times that had come with 9/11. My mom and aunt supported my decision to continue attending school, even if it was through online courses from home. The fear of being on campus as a Muslim female drove me to stay at home more often. I was fine with being a hermit for a while because I didn't want to be disturbed or brought out of my *Comfort Zone*. I simply buried myself in my studies, and that became my escape from the ever-piercing gaze of the world looming over Muslims.

Labor of Love

Sully, my first child, was born on October 7, 2001. This also happened to be the day that the United States invaded Afghanistan to bomb Osama bin Laden's terrorist cell. I had mostly spent the nine months prior in bed or in the hospital getting fluids because my hyperemesis gravidarum (extreme nausea) had gotten so bad. My diet consisted of bland noodles and Gatorade. I always wondered if you could actually produce a human being with such an unhealthy diet. It turns out that you can!

After two days of difficult labor, a perfect little human made his arrival into the world. It was love at first sight; unconditional in every sense. Once all of the family visits had ended and I was finally alone with my son, I put my thumbs in each of his tiny hands. He instinctively held on tightly. I lifted him slightly, and his head rolled back, allowing him to look up at me. Even as a newborn, he was strong, perfect, and 100 percent dependent on me. My life had changed in an instant, and this time change had come in the form of a seven-and-a-half pound human being.

While I was admiring my son, I heard the word "Afghanistan" mentioned on the television that was hanging from the corner of the room, so I turned the volume up. The news reporter was talking about "Operation Enduring Freedom" and the nighttime bombing campaigns that were going to cripple the Taliban regime supporting Osama bin Laden.

In a moment of irony, I remembered all of the people in school that used to mistake Afghanistan for Africa. Those people, and many more around the world, would never have that problem again. Afghanistan was coming into worldview, but not for the reasons one would hope. We were known for terrorists and the Taliban, the top two worst things in America. Anything positive about Afghanistan was light years away, and there were times I wished I *had* come from Africa.

I remember turning off the TV so that I didn't have to hear or think about death and destruction in a moment when I had been blessed with a little life. I swaddled Sully tightly in the pink and blue striped hospital blanket and cradled him in my arms. My emotions were all over the spectrum, as I was happy to be holding him but sad about the world he was being born into.

Sully had no idea, but at only a few hours old, his identity as a Muslim male was already considered negative in the world. I prayed to God that he would always be healthy and that he wouldn't have to be ashamed of who he was or where his parents came from. I hoped I could protect him and keep him safe from all the external forces I knew I had no control over. I cried mixed tears of joy and sorrow, with some of the tears falling onto his little chest. Kissing his forehead, I made up my mind to do whatever my mama bear instincts required in order to protect him and raise him to be a good person. Regardless of the deck that had already been stacked against his life, he was now my sole purpose.

$100 Perfection

Right after the hospital discharged me, I drove straight to my mom's gas station. Dad was sitting behind the counter at the cash register. He couldn't climb stairs or walk long distances anymore, so he had not been able to visit me or Sully at the hospital. Weighing in at less than 100 pounds, Dad shuffled to meet us halfway from the door. His illness had made him more emotional, so he did not hesitate to break into tears when he saw Sully. He gingerly leaned over the car seat and softly kissed the baby. Then, with pure joy in his eyes, he hugged me and said, "Oh my God, he is perfect." And just for a moment, I knew his pain had lifted, leaving him in a peaceful state.

In customary Afghan fashion, Dad removed a crisp 100-dollar bill from the cash register and put it on the side of the car seat, right under Sully's blanket. He was honoring the only grandchild he had, and for the next few months, Sully would find his place in his grandfather's lap, where he was most happy and spoiled as a baby.

Unforgettable Apologies

Looking out the window of Dad's hospice room brought back memories of our family trips and his favorite spot, *Sari Zameen*. The room was situated on the west side of the building, where I could gaze upon the beautiful pink and orange sunset over the navy blue Rocky Mountain range of Colorado. In that moment, I wanted nothing more than to turn back the clock to a time when my family and I were together inside our white minivan.

Turning my face back to Dad, I found him lying stiff and pale on the hospital bed. Instantly, I felt like I was in a horror movie. I walked toward him and sat in the white visitor's chair beside his bed. The chair and bed smelled sterile, like the rest of the room, and I couldn't help but to think about how his life would have been if he had stayed in Afghanistan. I held his hand carefully, so I wouldn't hurt his frail body, and sat in quiet denial.

My son, who had spent most of his short life inside hospitals, was not with me that day. I wasn't allowed to bring him because nine months is too young to be allowed in a place of death and sadness. It was just me, my thoughts, and our fading warrior. I wondered when I would wake up from this nightmare and find my dad cancer-free, teaching Sully how to box in the ring like the champions.

He awoke in pain, his sliver of eyes barely able to see that I was the only one in the room. "Nooria, Nooria, Nooria," he cried out.

"*Padar*, it's me, Niggin. Mommy is at the gas station, but she will be here soon."

The morphine drip was attached to his hand, and I wondered if he was in some other world where he and Mom were together. The nurses walked in to check on him, and he became more conscious. He began to cry and yell, "I am so sorry. Please forgive me for the trouble I put you through. I am so sorry. I am so sorry."

"Tell him it's our job. He doesn't have to apologize for anything," the nurses replied, unsure of why he was apologizing to them.

When the nurses left, he turned to me and said, "I'm sorry, Niggin. I'm so sorry, Niggin."

Too emotional to respond, I simply held his hand and cried with him. When my throat finally cleared, I spoke up. "*Padar*, don't be sorry. We love you so much."

Still, he continued apologizing, and every one of his apologies broke my heart and battered my soul all the more. I just wanted him to stop. I continued to kiss his hand and assure him that he had done nothing wrong, but he must have been fighting battles in his head that I couldn't see. I heard some crying coming from the room next to Dad's and curiously peeked over from the doorway. To my surprise, the two nurses that had been working with Dad were sobbing over his apologetic statements. Two hospice nurses crying over a dying patient? It further confirmed my belief that he had a heart of gold.

My aunt, along with some of my cousins, showed up with Mom later that afternoon, and once again there was a flurry of life in that tiny room of death. My aunt had flown in from California earlier that day. Mom had called Dad's family earlier that week, giving them the news that no one wants to hear. The reality of how close he was to the end of his life hit us all hard. How do you say goodbye to someone who has given you so much to remember?

As soon as my aunt saw my father's frail state, she began crying and kissing his hands and face. A tiny woman herself, she let out a heart-shattering cry. "*Shayerjan*, I am here. I am here, little brother." It was as if Dad had been waiting for the sound of her voice, because as soon as he realized it was his sister, he took his final breath, and let go of the life he had fought so hard to hold onto. Instantaneously, I was alone in the world again.

High on Motherhood

I found joy in being a mother. The sheer act of being at another human being's beck and call is a humbling act of selflessness. I could now empathize with my parents and their struggles with raising us. Believing I was stuck in my marriage for life, I decided it was time to have another child so that I could continue on the path of motherhood, since it suited me so well.

My second child, Eeman, was born two years after Sully. My hyperemesis gravidarum returned, making me just as sick bringing her into this world as I had been with him. I missed Dad and felt immense sadness at the fact that he was not around to see his second grandchild come into the world. The emotional stress of his death and my condition made it so that I ended up staying with Mom most days.

I willingly disconnected from the world around me, avoiding even basic conversation with Shabir. I was never sure what version of him I was going to get, and it was easier to hide in the *Comfort Zone* than to fix a relationship that was broken to begin with. The problem was further exacerbated by the fact that Shabir was at the peak of experiencing full-blown bipolar disorder symptoms and extreme psychosis episodes, as he had stopped working his traditional job and taking his medications as directed. Because my family did not have experience with formal mental health issues, as is true of most Afghan families, we often dismissed Shabir's "strange behavior" as stress.

Although the résumé of my life says I grew up in America, I had been very sheltered from the influences of the world, so drugs and alcohol were as foreign to me as sunscreen. One afternoon, Mom decided to come over and visit me because she had heard family members mention that Shabir was acting "crazy." She knocked on the door, and since I was taking a shower, she was met by her nephew who answered the door inebriated. Mom's childhood hadn't been picture perfect like mine, so she knew what he was up to and began to lecture him on how irresponsible he had become.

When I came out of the bathroom and saw Mom angrily staring at Shabir across the living room couches, I knew something was wrong. She glared at me as I stood there with my hair dripping wet and my face looking extremely lost. Before I could say anything, she started yelling at me. "How could you be so *beaaqel* ["stupid" in Dari] and not know that he has been smoking all day? How could you not know what weed smells like? What else is he doing behind your back?"

All I could think was, *Why in the world is Mom yelling at me?*

Then I remembered that a couple of nights before Mom's untimely visit, Shabir had opened a package and dumped its contents onto our small dining table. He began to explain that the four bags on the table were doctor recommended "relaxing herbs" from Hawaii. It was a more natural way to treat his stress. I was so naïve that I really believed him. There they were on the table, four bags of "relaxing herbs" beautifully wrapped and sealed with my ignorance.

The Writing on the Wall

I squinted my eyes open to find the LED of the alarm clock glaring back at me like it was angry that I was awake at such an ungodly hour. It was 3:05 a.m., and I had been awakened by the smell of burning wax and voices coming from my living room. *Who is at our house at this hour, and what in God's name is that smell?* I wondered. Eeman had fallen asleep next to me while I was nursing her, so I moved her from my bed to her crib on the opposite side of my room.

Stumbling into the hallway, I noticed a flickering yellow light on the walls. As I moved closer to the living room, my eyes widened in the light of hundreds of lit candles that had been placed all over the house. Every single hair on my body stood up, and cold chills ran down my spine when I peeked in the room and found Shabir having a conversation with a blank computer screen. Scared and curious all at once, I moved closer to him and realized that the walls of our apartment had been covered with red permanent marker. The writing didn't make sense to me, because it looked like mathematical equations mixed in with religious text in Arabic. To top it all off, our stereo speakers had somehow made their way into the fish tank. Sitting on the closest chair, I had to pinch myself to make sure I wasn't dreaming up the scene or watching the movie *A Beautiful Mind*.

When Shabir noticed me, he whispered, "The house is bugged, so I had to turn off the lights. Also, look over there." He pointed out our balcony door. "The FBI is sitting in that building across the street. They're videotaping us, so go cover yourself." In that moment, I was a freaked out little girl. I had no idea what to do. I figured there was no right answer, so I simply sat on the couch and watched the conversation continue between Shabir and the computer screen. I called his family over the next morning, and they helped clean up the wax-drenched carpet and destroyed furniture. As I was picking the solid wax out of the carpet, I wondered if Shabir would ever be stable again. That day was the start of a never-ending cycle of treatment and relapse.

23

Dirty Little Secrets

While mental health problems are nothing to be ashamed of, I had no idea what I was dealing with. Shabir's family treated him with religious anecdotes and discouraged him from hanging out with his "bad friends" who gave him drugs that further aggravated his lack of mental stability. No one wanted to believe that he was ill or that there was a science behind how to deal with it. It was either the drugs or the devil's work, but there was no way that it could be something psychological. All the while, my children and I were stuck in the middle of hospital visits and family meetings until each episode would pass and he would be stable for another few days.

As Shabir became more unstable, I became angrier. My family members were praising me for being an "angelic" wife and for putting up with him and his illness. I sat there smiling quietly while suffocating under the weight of their comments. I felt like a sacrificial lamb, overpowered by the traditions and decisions of my elders. I spent a lot of time thinking about how I had arrived at that place in my life, and I came to the realization that for years I had been fake smiling through a life that others had envisioned for me. In truth, there was no honor in keeping myself and children in an unsafe situation with an unstable person, but I stayed because I felt it was the right thing to do. I was consoled by persuading myself that this was a test from God, and all I had to do to pass the test was to hang on to the little sanity I had left.

The Good Muslim Girl and the Predator

As a student, I was quite proud of my ability to research a subject until I had the answers, so I figured I would treat my spiritual life the same. Maybe there were others who were more knowledgeable about life and its challenges that could help me understand the struggles of my journey. I sought advice from "Muslim" scholars and was often met with very sexist and gender-phobic answers about what a "good Muslim girl" should do in my situation. Still wanting to do what felt right within my heart, I continued to seek answers.

I can recall one particular life-changing moment where I approached an Imam while in California for an Islamic-focused conference. (An Imam is to Muslims what a priest is to Catholics.) One of my cousins recommended I speak with him because he had helped her in the past, and she believed he was a good person. I found him after attending a workshop he had facilitated and asked if I could consult him on a very important life matter. There was a line of people also seeking his advice, so I felt really appreciative when he agreed to spend a few moments with me.

We moved away from the crowd to a secluded corner of the hotel lobby, and I began to explain my marital situation. As I spoke, the Imam moved closer to me, popping the invisible bubble of my personal space. I tried to brush it off, but then he looked at me in a way that made me feel very uncomfortable, and I found myself struggling to complete my sentences. He placed his hand on the wall beside my head and I felt the heat exuding from his arm. The next thing I knew, he was asking me some very strange questions about my sex life. "Have you been masturbating? How do you attain pleasure in the relationship? You are an attractive woman. Is your husband attractive too?" While I didn't think any of his questions were relevant to my situation, the naïve part of me assumed that he was asking with good intent.

It didn't take long before my intuition was kicking me in the face, and it soon became clear to me that his intentions were not as good as I had thought. His voice started to fade, and white noise entered my head. I was somewhere between getting ready to throw up and passing out, when I forced myself to snap out of the moment. *What the heck is happening? What the hell am I still doing here?*

The Imam said something and then laughed. The next thing I heard was, "Do you want to go with me to my car, where we can have a deeper conversation about your marriage problems?" Very quickly, I made an excuse that I was late meeting my cousin and had to leave. When I finally found my cousin, I told her about the incident. She apologized for the situation, and we moved on with our day as if nothing had happened.

In a state of confusion, I flew back to Colorado that evening and didn't tell anyone about my experience for a very long time. I was embarrassed and wanted nothing more than to sweep it under the rug like it had never happened. I forgot his name and his face in hopes that I would never hear it mentioned in my presence again, yet I am choosing to highlight this story for a couple of reasons.

Let's Pry Open the Can of Worms

First, I would like to emphasize that the sexual objectification of women is prevalent around the world, regardless of religion and culture. Out of every five American women, one has experienced sexual assault. The statistics for sexual harassment are even worse. That's a big problem that requires a forum for discussion not only in America but on the world stage, where one out of every three women experience sexual abuse. That's 1.3 billion women.

I later found out that the Imam I had been speaking to had been released from his position in his community for making similar sexual advances on other younger women. I kicked myself so hard for not writing a letter to the conference community and speaking out against his behavior when it occurred. I really wanted to and had even brought myself to draft the letter, but I was too scared and ashamed of what had happened, so I never sent it.

My story is also a reminder that even though I was fully dressed in baggy clothes with my hair covered in a headscarf, *this still happened to me*. As a lot of victims of sexual harassment or assault tend to do, I thought that maybe I had said something wrong or that I had misunderstood the Imam. The voices of accusation against myself were loud. I kept taking showers, hoping to clean my mind and erase the layer of dirt he had added to my life story. Later, when I decided to deal with the impact this situation had on me, I realized that *he* was the one who was wrong. *He* was in a position of trust, and *he* had taken advantage of me during a very vulnerable time in my life.

By sharing my story here, I hope to give others permission to break out of the self-blame cycle. Self-blame turns into self-shame, leaving us emotionally paralyzed. Consequently, we become stuck in the *Comfort Zone*, scared to face our pain. Stories must be told in order to educate others about what sexual misconduct looks like and how often it happens in our communities. More importantly, women need to support each other and encourage each other to speak out about these taboo topics, especially in patriarchal cultures where women are taught to be *silent people pleasers*.

I am not a psychologist or therapist, but I have worked with sexually abused children, and I could see signs of mental health issues on all sides of the story. From the victim to the perpetrator, there was a cycle of abuse that had to be broken by lots of treatment and therapy, and it usually started with someone acknowledging there was a problem. It was all over the reports I read in child welfare cases and usually the story was that the perpetrators had been abused as children themselves. Somewhere along the way, the perpetrators were encouraged to repeat the acts that had been committed against them or they were not corrected about how to treat others. And so, not only their lives, but the lives of many others, ended up in ruins. As the saying goes, "Hurt people hurt people."

Sometimes I hear people say, "Nope. The woman must have done something to provoke him [referring to men in general]," or someone will make a comment such as, "She must have dressed like a slut," or "She wears a lot of makeup. She must have been trying to seduce him." Their comments lead me to believe that the objectification of women is a far bigger problem than any of us want to admit. As a Multi-American woman who identifies as both Afghan and Muslim, there are many uncomfortable conversations in my family about the biases we carry about women. Males are treated with more respect and typically given more freedom to explore their talents in Afghan culture, so I grew up thinking that men were worthier of social privilege and financial power. As a mother, I realized that I had to be the one to break the cycle of limiting beliefs by teaching my children to question what their relatives and friends say about women. I want my children to think differently and develop new ideas that will bring about gender equity.

Feminism-isms

Feminism can be defined and interpreted in so many different ways that I constantly find myself weighing the American perspectives of feminism against my own broad perspective that is an enmeshment of American and Afghan values. The subjugation of women—a dominant theme from both a global and historical perspective—can also be defined in many ways, depending on a person's worldview. Because the sociopolitical position of women within each culture is different, the subject of feminism must be addressed by female leaders in those parts of the world. Furthermore, the feminist movement should be seen as a progression of *human* rights, not a "one size fits all" approach to defining a woman's role within any given society.

Women in America, for example, have the right to vote, to own a business or work in most industries, and to make choices about their bodies (Well, mostly depending on the political administration in charge). The Western view of feminism supports the full participation of women in society, and the political narrative on women's rights seems to dominate mainstream media's attention. This did not happen overnight though. It came about in phases or *waves* that measured the experience of women against that of their male counterparts, and when discrepancies were found, women (and some men) fought to bring about change.

In other parts of the world like Afghanistan, women continue to battle for rights on a more fundamental level. Because the narrative is very patriarchal, a woman's husband or family members will dictate how she should dress, how she should act, and whether she should have children or not. Even if women are technically "allowed" certain rights like voting, they are discouraged by family and cultural norms from participating. Sometimes a woman may be asked to side with her husband's opinions, as if she is only an extension of her partner's voice. So, being a feminist in a place like Afghanistan is simply asking to exist as a human being; a vast difference from the progressive American perspective.

Because I have sons, a husband, and a father who raised me well, I have a hard time accepting the extreme feminist narrative about excluding the voices of males altogether in order to achieve equality in the sociopolitical standing of women across the world. This world is split almost equally between those that identify as females and males, so any progress in regard to healing and bringing about equality will require effort from both dominant gender groups.

Women do not need to *dominate* the world, but *virtuous people* must prevail. I could sit here and argue that women make better leaders than men because women are by essence more nurturing human beings, but that is beside the point! It is the job of parents to teach their sons and daughters that both narratives are valid, create dialogue around the importance of sharing stories, and encourage autonomy in the family dynamic. That is what will produce the kind of virtuous people our world so badly needs.

Most importantly, in order for women to abandon the cycle of self-blame or a victim-based mentality, men must become allies by creating an environment where the narratives of women are welcome and encouraged. If something doesn't feel right, women must say something—or in today's age, post something! While I say this from the perspective of a very American woman, I have true respect and admiration for the women around the world who risk their lives by speaking out against injustice and the lack of equality.

True feminism is not in the portrayal of *American women ripping off their shirts and shouting at oppressive men*, at least not from my perspective. True feminism is about increasing the narrative of women by creating an environment where women are encouraged to speak up, and all genders are partners in progress of virtue and equality.

Okay, let me step off of my soapbox so that we can return to my story.

Actions Trump Words

"*What you do speaks so loudly, that I cannot hear what you say.*"
~*Ralph Waldo Emerson*

From then on, I started questioning every text I read and challenging every idea that did not make sense to me. Furthermore, I chose to seek answers only from female scholars. I also continued digging around to research other faiths so that I could speak with clarity about why I was a Muslim. The path I had been on had taught me the *how* but never the *why*, and what I had failed to realize was that it was the *why* that mattered most. It became clear to me how ignorant I had been a few years earlier to believe that wearing the headscarf somehow made me more superior than others or that I could connect with God solely through my external appearance.

Now What?

My heart was aching for answers, but I had returned to square one. School was on hold until I could figure out how to become financially and emotionally stable, and I was in an unhealthy relationship with little to no communication or accountability. While Shabir's family was present and supported me by providing a place for me and my two children to stay, no one really understood the grave changes that were occurring around or within me. I was technically a single mom, experiencing an identity crisis, and moving around from apartment to apartment in hopes of stabilizing just enough to catch my breath.

One day, Shabir ended up going to Pakistan on a whim. I wasn't sure if it was a religious calling or if he just wanted to be left to be alone to self-medicate, but I found myself back with Mom, and I did not want to leave. I was lucky to have her. It was obvious that she was experiencing some guilt regarding the harsh reality that had become my life at such a young age. This was probably not what she had imagined for either of us, and all those fears she had years ago about taking sides in the family had become her reality.

While Mom had been renting a house from an acquaintance, she was not happy living in someone else's home. One day, when we were conversing about where she and my siblings were going to live next, we had a moment of clarity. She had a stable income, and my credit rating was still intact—because the credit card companies hadn't caught up to my deteriorating financial situation yet—so we decided to partner together to buy a new house. It was something of a surprise and an unexpected blessing that would assist us both in major transitions that would happen in the next few years.

When Shabir returned to America, I picked him up from the airport. On the way home, I casually mentioned that the kids and I were now living with Mom in our new house. Thinking I was joking, he looked at me and started laughing. When I told him I was serious, he stared off into the distance again, his face indicating that he was not happy. No proud Afghan male would ever move into his mother-in-law's house and still be able to feel like the man of the house. Shabir eventually moved us out of Mom's house and into another apartment, but in my heart I knew that I would come back our house someday.

Shortly after moving back in with Shabir, the reality of my life hit me again. Emotional and physical exhaustion crept in, and appearing strong and unaffected became more and more difficult. The challenges lived somewhere between who I believed I was and who I wanted to be in life, but the fog in my head made it difficult for me to see the rough patches ahead.

Guys, seriously. Just shut up and listen for just a minute.

As Shabir and I continued to drift apart, I daydreamed about finding inner peace with God. After one of my endless rants to God about seeking answers to questions about my faith and spirituality, I read about a retreat for women at a secluded mosque deep in the desert mountains of New Mexico. The retreat had been started by a group of women who would meet yearly to learn from each other. While the mosque never became the center of a thriving community as the founder had hoped, it served as a stunning location for spiritual rejuvenation. The retreat was scheduled for the day after I had read about it, so I dropped everything I was doing and ran to Shabir, begging him to let me drive there with his sister that night.

In my adamant determination to find inner peace, I made it to New Mexico. I still remember the long drive. It took twice the time it should have, but the roads to our destination were winding and filled with forest views and long stretches of desert, and the small towns we passed were decorated with authentic Southwestern decor.

We arrived on site at dusk and were met by a beautiful group of women who identified my cousin and I as "those young Afghan girls from Denver." Most of them couldn't believe that we had trekked there by ourselves. As fate would have it, the speaker that had come to enlighten the group was the Iranian-American Muslim author Laleh Bakhtiar. Not only was she a modern American clinical psychologist, but she was also a scholar of Islam and a mother. She told us many interesting stories, but when she shared about how she had spent seven years in isolation to dedicate herself to the scientific translation of the Quran, it was like my prayers had been answered.

Laleh challenged the group's perception of women in religion, arguing that the translation of chapter four, verse 34 in the Quran had been misinterpreted for more than 1,400 years. The traditional translation from Yousef Ali (one of the world's most popular translations of the Quran) reads as follows:

"As to those women on whose part ye fear disloyalty and ill-conduct, admonish them (first), (Next), refuse to share their beds, (and last) beat them (lightly)."

The Arabic word *daraba*, which was translated by Youself Ali to mean "beat them lightly," has six pages worth of possible meanings. Instead of husbands being allowed to beat or cause harm to their wives, as most men believe the verse advocates, Laleh instead provided the translation, "Husbands should *go away* or leave their wives in times of anger."

After all, it was more like the character of the Great Prophet Muhammad to treat others with respect and kindness. In religious stories about the Prophet, whenever he would face challenging times with his wives, he would leave their presence until he cooled off, and then he would return to them. His dislike of domestic violence was well documented, but this part of his story had been overlooked in the masculine translation.

While the Arabic language is complicated, and I am no linguist by any means, why would the majority of Muslims follow the more violent transliteration if the man who was the greatest example of the religion never partook in such behavior? As Laleh uncovered these truths, my eyes were opened to the possibility that the feminine narrative was missing from Islam because women scholars were not as prevalent as men.

Laleh also taught me that the word *Kafirun*, translated in English to mean "infidel," was actually rooted in the Arabic word for "ungrateful." Was it possible that we had been wrong all along about labeling people as Muslim or non-Muslim based on our own definitions? Who were we to include or exclude people based on a set of criteria so focused on external actions? There is a whole world in the heart of each human that none of us can see into. If that is where true spirituality lives, then who are any of us to judge others by how they express their devotion to God? As I sat there listening to her, a revelation hit me in the heart like a ton of bricks: *Words matter.*

Now, I am not a scholar of Islam, nor do I claim to have extensive knowledge about my faith, but I came to understand "Universal Islam" that day. I wasn't looking to turn my religion into something it wasn't; I was looking for the universal concept of Islam that I had been promised by God in the Quran. So what if my views were considered "Sufi-like" or not widely accepted by others? I was not concerned about what labels others wanted to place on my viewpoint. My focus was to find an interpretation of Islam that fell in line with all the stories I had read about who the Prophet Muhammad was as a human being.

That weekend, I spent a lot of time pondering what this meant for my spirituality and for me as a Muslim. The interpretation was unconventional, but it allowed me to stay curious about what "inclusivity" in Islam really meant. Why did Muslims make

Islam so exclusive that people who did not "show up" a certain way were "removed?" Why did the Muslim leaders of the world present such a violent view of Islam?

The *why's* started spinning in my head, culminating in a juxtaposition of moral clarity and fear of going against what I had been taught. I wasn't ready to go back to my life as I had known it. I was just starting to scratch the surface of internal essence, and I felt really vulnerable and restless. My life was changed, and I had a whole new perception of spirituality. I could now be a little more comfortable in my own skin because I knew that while the world could tell me how to act as a Muslim woman, I had a choice to believe what I wanted to about God. I could be authentic, even in my faith, because it was my behavior and self-reflection that mattered.

Being in the *Authenticity Zone* allowed me to expand my tolerance and acceptance of others, but I had to first have the courage to accept myself. I wanted to stay in New Mexico and feed off of the soul food that had been presented to me, but the weekend was over. My cousin and I jumped in the car to return to reality, unaware that the question of human life would be handed to me, and that instead of being in the eye of the storm, I was about to face the destructive winds on the outside.

Butterflies

I turned off the car and sat quietly in the driver's seat for a moment. February was always cold in Colorado, so I checked the back seat of the car to make sure that Sully and Eeman were still bundled up and sleeping. By this time, P.J. was long gone, and I was sitting in a four-door sedan that I had refused to name. Cars had always provided me sanctuary, but a sharp wind from the east shook the sedan from side to side, breaking up my hopes of spending any more time in the quiet solace of the parking lot. The clouds in the sky were growing darker and getting closer, as snow flurries started hitting the windshield. There was no time to ponder my latest dilemma. A snow storm was coming, and I had to get inside before the temperature dropped and the babies felt the cold.

I found a way to power through carrying the groceries into the house along with my three-year-old son in one arm and one-year-old daughter in the other. The two little humans I carried in my arms had changed homes so many times in the short span of their lives that they were used to me lugging them around. The realization of how instability had impacted their development weighed heavy on my heart, but it quickly dissipated when a sharp burst of wind hit my face. *They will be okay,* I thought to myself. *We will all be okay, somehow.*

After I had managed to strategically place the groceries on the floor without jostling the babies around too much, I brushed the snow off their jackets and took them to my room to lie down on my bed. When I went back to the living room, Shabir entered the house in a frenzy, asking me if I wanted to go to California with him and one of our aunts. I knew it wasn't a good idea, but I entertained any prospect of adventure, especially if it meant going back to a place I considered home. Instantly, I began dreaming of returning to the California sunshine I had grown up with. Maybe this was the opportunity for me find the happiness I had as a child. Within a week, we were all packed up and on our way to California.

Although the adventurer in me wasn't scared to face the unknown, I became terrified at the thought of revealing to my family (especially my mom) that I was pregnant again. A cloud of guilt loomed over my head for having been careless about birth control. The thought of my mother's disappointment made it so that I could hardly breathe. We had decided to move to California so quickly that I figured it was best to hold the announcement until I was far away from her piercing, judgmental eyes, but the time had come to make the dreaded call.

"Hi, Mom...Yes, we made it. Um, so I have something to tell you." As the conversation continued and my secret was revealed, she emitted her infamously loud sigh over the phone, just like the one I had heard during the high school play many years prior. My heart sank to the ground.

As predicted, Mom was extremely disappointed. She knew how unhappy I was in my marriage, so this was pretty much a tragedy of epic proportions from her perspective. It also didn't help that I was far away from her and any help she could provide. The laser beams of her judgmental eyes morphed into piercing words of disappointment, making their way through the phone and into my heart. I wanted to disappear from the world.

When the news got out, many extended family members called me hinting that I should consider an abortion. Shabir was "sick," so what good would another child bring to me or my failing relationship? I was at a crossroads again, and to make matters worse, I was facing a moral dilemma about how to deal with the life that was growing inside of me.

The Comfort of Babies and Sheet Caves

There I was, in a tiny bedroom in the middle of a city I hardly knew, lying on top of my mattress. Although I was accompanied by the warm sun and my two children, I felt like I was in the deep, dark cave of my life again. I covered myself with sheets so that no one could see me. I wanted to escape the horrible thoughts that were ruminating in my soul. I had become exceptionally skilled at punishing myself with negative self-talk, and this moment was yet another battle in the war against myself.

I remember trying to define what a third child really meant to me at that point in my life. As my puffy red eyes peeked through the cocoon I had created, my eyes fell upon my two toddlers playing together not too far away from me. They were exploring the room and babbling to one another in their own language. Innocent and faultless, their laughter filled the relatively empty room with love. They had no idea that violent storms were brewing in my heart and mind.

With every gust of guilt that blew through my mind, my lungs would tighten, restricting air to my body. The tears rolled slowly from my cheeks to the floor where the babies played. *"Sully...Ee-*

man," I called. *"Biya eenja* [Dari for 'come here']." They both giggled and scurried over to me without hesitation, jumping into the bed and freeing me from my cocooned state. I pulled them into the bedsheets with me, and we became one big jumble of love.

That day, in a small California apartment, my children grounded me in a time of sadness in the same way that I had comforted Mom in her time of sadness—except there was no Bugs Bunny or siren lights in the background this time. It was just me with my babies in the sheets. With my arms full and my face buried in baby cheeks, I started to remember how lucky I was to be in the presence of two tiny human beings that would someday turn into dreamers and travelers like their mom. Their eyes were beaming with light, and the specks of light brown inside of their dark brown eyes were sparkling. Even though my hug lasted a little too long and they squirmed to get away from me to continue their exploration, I was experiencing another life-changing moment.

My role as a mother was not only the most important role I had, but it made me a stronger human being from every other perspective. My children brought out my mama bear instincts. I would do anything to protect them, like Dad and Mom protected us when we were younger. There is nothing more authentic than the expression of unconditional love in the simple moments that shape our identities for the future.

Others in my family saw my pregnancy as a flaw, but the narrative beaming from my soul was quite the opposite. This child's life was a gift that I needed to accept and take responsibility for. If I could be so careless to create physical life without precaution, I needed to be responsible for the outcome. Love breeds love, and I loved my children more than anything in the world. An abortion was not the right choice for me. I saw my babies as individuals and did not tie them to my relationship or failure of it. They were an entity and life force all on their own, and if guided virtuously, they could change the world someday.

In the *Authenticity Zone*, I made a decision that was true to who I was and the circumstance I was in. It was one of the best decisions I have ever made because the life I brought into this world continues to be the light of our family. Maryam knows she was an "oops" baby, but I also tell her she was a *"wow"* baby because she is an artist with a soul that beams of light and energy.

In the same moment that I decided that abortion was not my path, I wondered if maybe…just maybe a divorce was. The only constant theme in my life at the time was my lack of authenticity and connection in my loveless marriage, where I was forced to deal with an array of mental health problems that were not under medical control. The theme of respect that I had previously tried to base my relationship on had not grown into love; instead, it grew into anger toward Shabir and my family. I resented my ancestral roots for putting me in this situation where I had to pretend that all was well in my world, and I allowed anger to penetrate my heart.

As a Muslim, I had been taught to be grateful for all the blessings I received in life, but I was confusing gratitude with unnecessary self-exploitation, something I now know that God doesn't expect of any human being. At this point, I had given up on trying to fix Shabir or our relationship. I was just going with the flow until I could come up with a plan. My heart was hurting for a better life for all of my children, including my unborn child, but I did not know how I was going to do it on my own or what a divorce would do to the family dynamic. For the moment, I didn't care; I just needed to rest. I ignored the smell of weed coming from the vents and the annoying arguments my aunt would have with her daughters. I stared out the window at the California sun and slept, knowing that the most important thing was getting through the next few months without falling apart completely.

Home Sweet Home

Within a couple of months, my children and I were back home with Mom again. My brother-in-law had come to fetch us because Shabir was having another episode and we needed a ride back to Colorado. On the drive back, my mind was consumed with negativity and anger toward myself for believing that moving to California would somehow bring me the happiness I had experienced as a child. I was physically exhausted from moving around all the time, and I realized it was up to me to take control and create stability for myself and my children. I wasn't going to wait around for Shabir to accept that he had a mental health issue, seek treatment, or decide to live his life differently. The only person I could control and change was myself, and believe me, this gal needed some serious work!

After Maryam was born, I spent a few months bonding with her and doing what I knew best: being a mom. She brought smiles to my face every day. When Maryam was eight months old, I officially entered the workforce so I could financially support our family. I say "officially" because my job was inside a corporate building with other people working the typical 9 a.m. to 5 p.m. schedule. Lucky for me (and for the corporation), I liked working. Like school, it was another escape.

Giving serious thought to divorce scared me, and making the divorce "official on paper" made me question my decision even more. I kept asking myself, *What will the children think when they're older? Will they hate me for making this decision? Am I doing some kind of disservice to my children by leaving their father?* As thoughts of uncertainty and fear crept into my head, I convinced myself that Shabir could get better. Maybe he would seek treatment and stop self-medicating, and we could find common ground again. Besides, how could I leave a man who was ill and suffering? What kind of human being picks up and leaves when times become rough?

I continued to punish myself as I made false promises to both myself and my family that I was going to file for divorce and move on. "Tomorrow, yup, tomorrow I am going to the courthouse," I would say. Even though I lived at home with Mom and the children, I went with the kids to see Shabir once a week. I often exaggerated any progress he had made, because I wanted to justify my reasons for staying in the relationship even though I knew it wasn't right. Things were supposed to change, but they hadn't. I was scared of the unknown and wanted to avoid dealing with the pain of a divorce.

I thought about Grandmother *Kokojan* and how she and my grandfather were separated but never divorced. Maybe that would work for us. It would make my life easier, and I could avoid any consequences of being on my own, because I could stay with Mom and live in this "in-between" state. Fear was in the driver's seat again, and I had agreed to become a backseat passenger, but we were driving backwards instead of progressing as I kept convincing myself that I could do it on my own.

I became a living, breathing ping pong ball in the game of life, living at home one year and moving back in with Shabir to try to work things out the next. During this time, Mom and my siblings became very frustrated with me. One day I would cry, tell them how unhappy I was, and vow to change my life, and the next I would ask for help with moving my stuff into a new apartment.

I was really good at making others happy; I knew how to do that well. I believed that if I could just focus on one day at a time, I could avoid dealing with the elephant-sized emotions that were growing inside my soul. What I did not realize is that emotions of that magnitude can easily become uncontrollable and will manifest themselves in other ways, appearing whenever they want to, raw and unrelenting. There was a metamorphosis on the horizon, and though I knew it was going to be painful and long, I also knew that somehow I would emerge from my cocoon and be able to fly on my own.

26

Destiny, by Little Shahira

My mother taught me how to be a single mom. After my father's death, she sold her business but continued to work long hours from home processing medical bills. While taking on other part-time jobs with different companies as a side hustle, she had figured out a way to keep her four children and three grandchildren together under one roof. My mom became the rock we all needed to hold onto during the storm that was life at the time. Mom sheltered us, fed us, kept us safe, and became a model of success that we would all learn to follow. I was so proud and lucky to call her my mom.

When I was in the fourth grade, my teacher asked my class to draw what we wanted to be when we grew up. It was no Picasso or anything, but I had drawn a curvy, curly-haired stick figure in a black business suit and red high heels. The woman was standing in front of a big corporate building with black window panes, wearing a crooked smile with a briefcase scribbled into her hand. That successful businesswoman in the picture was a mashup of myself and my mom, working for the company she had been so successful at when we lived in California.

My mom was a smart businessperson and completely independent. Though not as lively as Dad in her mannerisms, she was still the same adventurer who had once played with snakes and dragonflies, and I wanted to be her. Like a self-fulfilling prophecy manifesting itself, I found career success working for the same company I had drawn in the picture; the same one my mom had worked at many years before.

Entering the workforce was a difficult process, and there were times that I came home crying because I missed my children. This was my first traditional job, and the separation anxiety was difficult to cope with. It took me a while to be able to leave in the mornings without feeling guilty. When I made it to work, I would call my mom and ask if the kids were up yet or what they had eaten for breakfast. During breaks and the lunch hour, I would stay on the phone with the kids until it was time for me to clock back in. My mom would assure me that everyone was fine and that she was teaching all three of them their ABC's and basic preschool skills. I would come home and the kids would hand me their latest finger painting artwork that usually had the word "Mom" and a heart somewhere in the picture. After the warm welcome from my kids, we would sit down for dinner as a family and talk about our day. We were establishing a routine as a family, and the outcome was stability for me and the children.

Black Pantsuit, Red Heels, and a Scarf

The corporate landscape was new to me, and so were the challenges that came in the form of difficult bosses, strict schedules, and working with people who didn't care about others. Other part-time jobs I had held in the past were simple back office jobs where I was left alone or worked primarily from home. I was now working for a large-scale healthcare company. My introverted hermit side felt threatened. Being around people made me nervous, and because I was the only Muslim woman in the company, that brought additional stares and uncomfortable moments. Thankfully, people's fears about working with me resided once they took the time to get to know me as a person.

What I enjoyed most about working there was the opportunity to help my coworkers become more successful. For example, if I was answering the phone and had to stick to an average call time, I would prep some notes while the customers were speaking to me. As a result, I would take double the calls others would take, and management began to notice. People naturally came to me for help on how they could improve, and I found joy in building partnerships and watching people reach their goals. I moved up the corporate ladder quickly, learning to delegate, navigate the political landscape, and leverage relationships to reach common goals.

Not all days were golden. Some days were full of gossip, bad reviews, or disagreements. There were times that I wanted nothing more than to stay at home in my comfortable introverted space and give the finger to some of the people I worked with. My mom gave me pep talks, and like a personal life coach, she would urge me to deal with issues instead of running from them. She would call me at work and remind me that people could not stand in the way of my success unless I allowed them to. She reminded me that I was smart and talented, and she gave me the motivation to continue when I needed it most. Everyone needs a cheerleader, and my mom was mine.

Taking a lesson from Mom, I also worked other part-time jobs. If there was a way to make money, I was going to try it. Setting goals and quickly achieving them fueled my passion to work hard and for the first time in my life, I felt like I was an individual with a career; not a woman who was just playing an assigned role. Throughout it all, my mom was in the background cheering me on and reminding me that I could do it.

Back to School Nights

Not long after I had started working, I began attending a nontraditional university for adults to pursue a bachelor degree in business. This allowed me to work during the day and spend four hours in a classroom one night a week. I did not know what I wanted to be when I "grew up," but I did remember that someone had once told me you can't go wrong with a business degree.

While I was building confidence and experience at work and school, I still wasn't dealing with any of my deep-seated emotions. An unstable volcano of emotions was brewing underneath the surface of my smile. I buried myself in work and schoolwork to make all the hurt go away. The battles in my head ensued, but I drowned them out with music, small talk, and reading textbooks into the wee hours of the morning.

Avoidance became my coping mechanism, and I was good at it. I was constantly running to the façade of the *Comfort Zone*. Being authentic is uncomfortable at times, and it requires a lot of honesty and self-reflection. I was not quite ready to face all of that. I just wanted to go on with my life, pretending that my marriage had never happened and that my children had been born via Immaculate Conception.

It is a very painful process to accept the hard truths in our lives, and I was so good at repressing my feelings that I avoided any self-talk about how I was feeling. Anger began to replace my happiness, and I guarded my ego by distancing myself from the truth. If I had gotten to this point in my life by doing all the things others wanted me to, I was about to "undo" them. I was going to show the world that I was done pleasing everyone else, but not in a productive way; in a very angry, "fuck you" kind of way.

Hijab

Let's talk about the hijab. The purpose of the hijab (the Arabic word meaning "covering") is to provide a representation of one's religious devotion through modesty. It is an act prescribed by God through the Quran, closely followed by many Muslim women. It is worthy to note that in some parts of the world, the hijab is worn by men and women. We also see head coverings in two other monotheistic religions with Catholic nuns and Orthodox Jewish women. Regardless of the religion, the theme is the same: covering of the hair is a representation of modesty and devotion to God through one's external appearance. While the act of covering up and being modest is considered a religious command, the question that remains is whether wearing the hijab is really a choice. Having heard it both ways, I decided that modesty was the key to the ruling on the subject of the hijab.

I have seen the hijab worn in many different ways. Some women wear a thin veil, others a thicker fabric. Some women choose to show bangs or expose their necks, while others completely cover their faces, only exposing their eyes. After much research, I concluded that the way a woman decides to cover herself is largely related to her culture, but the general understanding is that you should cover your head as a public statement of who you are and what you believe.

When you wear a headscarf in public, you become a walking, talking representation of Islam. Because wearing the scarf is the act of making a public statement about one's religion, the opposite is assumed when a woman decides to take it off. The removal of a hijab incites a variety of concerns from others within the Muslim community. Does this woman no longer subscribe to her religion? Why doesn't she want to be seen as a Muslim anymore? While the reasons for why a woman decides to "unveil" can vary, this is generally viewed as a point of failure for a Muslim woman.

The subject of "uncovering" or removing the hijab is very taboo in both my religion and the Afghan culture. Some women in my family had decided to take theirs off. This was viewed as a disgraceful act in the eyes of some family members, as well as the general Afghan community. Good girl gone bad, you say? "Why would you cover up and then let it all out?" someone once remarked to me. I had been present for some of those conversations in my earlier years and even engaged in lengthy debates with my family whenever this very personal issue presented itself for public scrutiny. Ironically, I was now in the spotlight debating with myself about whether or not I wanted to cover my head anymore.

It was springtime and Mom, Shabir, and I were shopping for kids' clothes at an outdoor mall. On that particular day, I was in the midst of a "ping pong" moment, deliberating how the day would end and whether I would get in the car and go home with my mom or go to my aunt's house with Shabir. While I was deep in thought, we walked into a store that had automatic doors. Because the weather was warm, all the stores had the air conditioning on blast, and you could feel a rush of wind in your face as the doors parted. My thin scarf was casually wrapped over my hair and draped over my shoulders Persian-style with my bangs exposed.

As we walked into the store, a rush of cool air blew the head-scarf off of my head and onto my shoulders. I stood still for a second, my feet planted on the ground, pondering my next move. My mother and Shabir were walking ahead of me, so they hadn't noticed the life-changing event that had just taken place a few feet behind them. *Why is this such a hard decision to make?* I asked myself. *Why am I not moving my scarf back onto my hair where it belongs?* A matter of seconds felt like years, as I tried to answer one of the most difficult questions of my life.

Instead of moving my hands toward my shoulders, my feet began to march into the store with my hands to my sides and my hair exposed. No one probably noticed but me, but I felt very rebellious in that moment. When Mom and Shabir realized I had fallen behind, they looked back at me and as I got closer to them, their eyes widened with concern.

"So, you're taking it off?" my mom asked.

I didn't respond. None of my responses would have satisfied her laser-beaming eyes and judgments in that moment. My bangs and streaked hair were messy and tangled, but I didn't care. No longer in the spiritual mindset for wearing the headscarf, I continued to march on silently. Shabir didn't say much. He only looked disappointed and expressed his disapproval under his breath. I didn't care about him in that moment. I didn't even want to be shopping with him that day.

While I was still having conversations with God—because those had never stopped—I was having them in a less traditional sense. They became less like trusting prayers and more like debates, where my emotions were presented as facts and God was like a parent listening to a hormonal teenager.

Over the next few months, friends I had within the Afghan or Muslim community started to keep their distance from me. Most of them stopped calling me, and some I stopped calling. Because I was no longer wearing the hijab, I didn't fit in anymore. I was traveling a road that made people uncomfortable. I felt like everyone in the community was already talking about Shabir as the religious hypocrite who was doing drugs, and I was the "poor sacrificial lamb" who was married to him. I was experiencing isolation, but this time I had brought it upon myself. Instead of feeling empowered by my decision, I went down the path of self-blame and negative self-talk once again.

The hijab was no longer serving its purpose on my head because I no longer wanted to stand out in the world. I wanted to fit in; to assimilate and avoid all the questions that came with wearing a headscarf. I wanted to slide under the radar for once and just be anonymous again. The overall response to the removal of my hijab made me feel like a failure, and I began questioning other areas in my life. Was I a good mom? A good employee? A good daughter? Taking my headscarf off had not necessarily provided freedom, only anonymity. I still had the same questions about who I was as a person. If I didn't belong to the world I had come from, where did I belong?

I had removed my hijab as quickly as I had put it on, and looking back, both experiences happened during very immature junctures of my life. Both times, I was trying to prove that no one could tell me what to do, and guess what? No one stopped me. After I removed the hijab, I realized that I had been using it as a crutch for avoidance behaviors and comfort. In fighting against my authenticity, I did things in haste and out of anger instead of making calculated or thoughtful decisions.

To this day, I have chosen not to put the headscarf on in public. Instead, I choose to wear it only when I am standing in formal prayer to God or when I enter a sacred space of devotion—regardless of whether the sacred space is a church, synagogue, or mosque. My relationship with God requires no intermediary, and I make my decisions based on my gut intuition, which is guided by a moral compass that is rooted in Islamic beliefs.

While I am supportive of women who choose to wear the hijab, I have chosen to express my faith in God through my daily actions and behaviors, as I embody the characteristics of compassion and inclusivity. Modesty can be expressed in more than how we dress, and I refuse to let one small part of my external appearance define my voice on religion and spirituality. Muslim women are *no different* than any other women, and it's time for us to accept our diversity in what we have to contribute to the world—with or without the hijab.

She Did What?

Stories of "the girl who removed her hijab" are usually painted over, blacked out, and redacted from the script. Why? Because it is not considered *good* for Afghan girls to grow up with dirt on their armor. For this Afghan girl, after years of my marriage being broken, put back together, and then broken again, I had decided that I was going to distance myself from my family by playing the part of a reborn teenager. I was 26 going on 16.

What's Moderation?

Having fun like it was 1999 became my new hobby, and I embraced a lifestyle of partying. My upbringing had led me to believe that a person can only be labeled as "good" or "bad." There was no room for the label "human" in between. I didn't want to be Niggin anymore (the Afghan name I associated to) so I found ways to become physically unrecognizable to my family and to myself. I had seen other Afghan and Middle Eastern girls with blonde hair during my trips to California and thought to myself that they did not look very Afghan or Eastern anymore. It was nothing less of a complete make-over, so I started with dying my hair. Over time my blonde highlights suddenly turned into a head full of platinum blonde hair. It became an expensive alteration, but there was no black hair in sight. Hair as dark as mine could only stay blonde if it were dyed every month, and I willingly paid the money as long as I didn't have to think about what life was like before blonde.

Along with the blonde hair came the lighter makeup for my face, and eye makeup that often brought me the compliment that I looked "exotic." The lighter my skin tone became, the less Afghan I felt, and I was able to blend into the partying crowd without being noticed or recognizable. There was a sense of freedom that came from anonymity, but it was accompanied with feelings of isolation and disconnect from my family and my painful past. Transforming into a lighter shade made me feel more American, and I decided I was done being Afghan.

As sadness and anxiety emerged from inside me, I did what no "good" Afghan usually does: I saw a therapist. Unsure of how to deal with the emotions that were building inside of me, I was secretly hoping that someone could give me all of the answers I sought in one session. Though my main criteria was to find a female therapist who was somewhat local, I had also searched my health insurance directory for names that sounded foreign because a foreigner would probably understand the cultural collisions I had been facing, and that would cut out half the story. After hours of searching to no avail, I settled on a young, white American woman.

I tried my best to reduce the majority of my woes into a 45-minute CliffsNotes version. While the therapist couldn't help me with my deep-seated identity crisis (mostly because I never gave her the chance), she did tell me that I was self-medicating through alcohol. *What?* I couldn't believe what I was hearing from someone who barely even knew me. I never went to see her again. How dare she make such a quick assumption about me after one session? She couldn't understand where I was coming from—no one did.

"Pills are Good"

Along with emotional destruction came physical destruction. The stress of not dealing with life's challenges and bottling up my emotions was catching up to me and causing me to "self-medicate" in other ways.

After I had undergone surgery to remove my tonsils, I found that one of the side effects of the medication caused me to sob like a child. When my mom called to tell me that Shabir was on his way to get me and bring me home, I broke down into loud sobbing. I didn't want to see him, but I wasn't able to drive by myself.

The nurse walked in as I hung the phone up with my mom. "You okay?" she asked as she handed me a cup of water.

"I think so," I replied, wiping my tears.

"Here is the prescription from the doctor. He says you can take up to two pills at a time for pain every four hours. Tonsillectomies usually take a month or so to heal, so you will need these to get through the next week."

And just like that, I found myself battling a new problem.

It is amazing how easy it is to get a prescription for pain pills and how well a person can function while being on them. The doctors continued to prescribe me pain pills, even after all the pain from the tonsillectomy had gone away. I was self-medicating again, but this time the pills literally made all the noise and voices in my head go away. If I took one, the chatter in my head faded away, and I could just stare at the TV or my computer screen and think about nothing. If I took a few, they kept me in a world of slumber where I didn't dream because the sleep was so heavy. I would sleep like a bag of rocks and wake up hours and hours later without noticing any time go by. In my world, there was nothing a strong cup of coffee couldn't fix. I was living the American dream, popping pain pills at night and stimulating through energy drinks and constant caffeination during the day.

The pills made me numb and no one suspected that I had a problem. If someone asked what was wrong because my sentences didn't seem well put together, or my eyes would give out in exhaustion, I would respond with, "I just had surgery a week ago, and my throat still hurts so I am taking some medication" I used that line for two months in a row. I did not want to admit it, but the therapist was right. I was self-medicating and probably dealing with some form of depression. The pain pills had become another form of escape from a life I was so fond of escaping.

My heart was torn as I stood in the middle of two identities. Anything that made me an Afghan woman, I painted over including my dark hair. Everything I thought was the version of the American me left me in isolation and sadness. I was a rebel without a cause, and I had tried everything......except for providing myself a quiet moment to reflect on the disaster that was my life. I distanced myself from my kids by working long hours and sleeping when I was home. On the rare occasion when I would come home from work early, I would kiss them like crazy and play with them until it was bedtime. They didn't have to know what was going on with their mom outside the walls of their home. All that mattered was that they were safe and sound inside. The joy in their faces was everything I needed to keep going from one day to the next because I convinced myself that my only responsibility to them was to provide financial stability.

In all of the confusion I never stopped talking or complaining to God. I would ask why I turned out to be such a horrible person and why I was not selected to be one of the good ones! I hadn't been a good representative of my faith or culture, and I was not the perfect angel I had hoped I would turn out to be. I thought to myself, *Dad is probably turning over in his grave! God—please don't tell him what is happening down here on Earth!*

28
Life and Death (Literally)

In true rebellious fashion, I bought a shiny, black Suzuki GSXR motorcycle that I adoringly called Suzy. Years ago on my 17th birthday, I asked Dad for a sport motorcycle, and he burst into laughter thinking I was joking. When he saw the seriousness in my face, he broke out the laser beam eyes and in a dismissive tone said, "Over my dead body, you can have one!" Unfortunately, that became a true statement. My father was no longer alive, and I wasn't going to let anyone tell me what to do.

To my exhilaration, riding a motorcycle was just as amazing as I had hoped it would be, and I was slowly becoming addicted to it. When I was on my sport bike, it was like pure meditation because I was excited, connected, and focused *only* on the road. I didn't have to think about my problems because if I wanted to live, I had to pay attention to where I was and where other people were on the road. I loved keeping my eyes out for upcoming curves to test my understanding of inertia. I always kept my eyes on where I wanted to go instead of the road in front of me.

Please understand, a girl on a motorcycle—let alone an Afghan girl who was a mother to three kids—was turning my family's brains upside down. I tried to sell them on the fact that riding was a therapeutic experience and that I needed to have something just for myself. They didn't buy my story. My family saw my life breaking into pieces and spiraling downward, and there was nothing they could do to put me back to the way I used to be. It didn't matter to me, because I didn't want to be put back together.

Mom—who admitted this to me much later in life—felt that my downfall was her fault, especially after I bought my motorcycle. She had felt that the marriage of her daughter to her nephew was a mistake, but she allowed it to happen, and because of her, my life was in shambles. She prayed for my lost soul five times a day during her ritual prayers and had her own conversations with God about why I had become the way I was. When I would pass by her while she would be praying on the ground, she would look up with a disheartened, motherly stare. I shrugged it off, refusing to admit to myself how much pain and discomfort her disapproval really felt inside my heart.

After becoming more skilled on the sport bike, I started to test my ability to stay focused at high speeds. Thinking I might want to become a motorcycle racer someday, I once sped up to 120 miles per hour while riding on the highway. There was a moment of freedom and confidence followed by pure fear that my kids would grow up without their mother. Realizing that I wasn't in a good state of mind, I slowed down to normal speeds. Toying with risk and death, I was abusing the privilege of time that had graciously been bestowed upon me. If something didn't change soon, I wasn't going to make it through this "teenage temper tantrum" mode.

The Intersection of Trains and Near Death

Generally, I wore professional business attire to my office, but this particular day felt like a jeans and black leather jacket kind of day, so I stuffed my fancier black pants into my backpack. Glancing at my watch, I realized that I was going to be late for my early morning meeting with my boss, so I grabbed my helmet and hopped onto Suzy.

I sped on the highway, but not too much. The summer sun was shining brightly, and the view to the west revealed the beautiful Rocky Mountains of Colorado. As I turned onto the main road that led to work, the lights began flashing to warn of an approaching train. The person in front of me in a navy-blue sedan with tinted windows started speeding up in an effort to cross the railway before the bars came down. If I wanted to get to work on time, I was going to have to follow that car through the ringing alarms.

At the last minute, the person in the car in front of me quickly slammed on his brakes. Maybe he had decided to play it safe after all? Regardless, I was not expecting him to stop short, and frankly, I was driving way too fast to avoid his car. Rubber eventually met the road when my bike hit the back of the sedan. I flipped off the bike and rolled onto the train tracks. For a brief moment, I stared up at the bright, blue sky before I looked to my left and saw a speeding locomotive coming toward me. Damn! I was going to be late for my meeting after all.

Luckily, the train was moving slower than my reaction time, and I was able to get up in enough time to run over to Suzy on the other side of the track. I lifted the 300-pound broken body of my motorcycle and walked it over to a store parking lot about 500 feet away. The navy car that had been involved in my accident was long gone. *What a low life piece of shit!* I thought. *What if I had been lying unconscious on the railroad track? Where is my apology for your last-minute decision that I almost caused me to die?* (Of course, it wasn't my fault for following too closely!)

I called my boss to let her know that I was going to be a little late for work and told her a brief version of my near-death experience. She rushed over to where I was and insisted I go to the hospital.

"I'll be fine!" I said, but she read through my bullshit when I almost fell over as I walked toward her.

When I arrived at the hospital emergency room, my left leg was so swollen that the hospital staff could not remove my riding boot. When they finally forced it off, I cried and yelled obscenities because of the pain. I asked the nurse, "If my ankle is sprained, how come I was able to move my 300-pound bike across the street?" She laughed and looked at my boss in amazement. I learned a lot about the power of adrenaline that day.

Although my motorcycle was out of commission for a while, one of my colleagues helped fix it back to normal. When my sprained ankle healed, I got back on and rode my bike again to prove that I was not afraid of one bad experience. However, something had changed because the rush I used to get while riding was not there anymore. Disappointed, I drove less and less until Suzy was in the garage more often than on the road.

It wasn't long before I gave up riding altogether. I had decided that if I wasn't responsible enough to safely ride a motorcycle, then there was no reason for me to put myself or others at risk. When I finally allowed myself to focus more on why I was really riding, I realized that the theme of avoiding my problems continued to prevail in my life. If I wanted an unobstructed view into my own heart, I had to take off the proverbial emotional helmet I had been hiding behind.

While I still miss Suzy some days, selling the bike and moving on at that juncture in my life allowed me to accept that there was a better way to deal with my problems. It also forced me to avoid escaping my emotions by jumping on my motorcycle. Instead, I started coming home after work again. I even helped my mom make dinner and would read a book to the children before putting them to bed. I wasn't the ideal Afghan daughter or mom, but I was returning to a routine that would help ground me again.

Don't get me wrong—I am still an avid fan of the motorcycle. I like to joke with my husband about buying a pair of matching bikes when we hit our 50s. Really though, I am only half joking, because now that I'm in a fresh headspace, I can trust that the next Suzy-mobile will be handled with less speeding, more gratitude for being alive, and a whole lot of fun!

DO NOT MESS WITH MOTHER NATURE

I almost met death again in another situation where this time I was humbled by nature. One hot summer afternoon, which also happened to be my 26th birthday, my extended family invited me and the kiddos to hang out near the river in the mountains. As much as I wanted to be away from family during the rough patches in my life, the mountains and rivers of Colorado always had a way of calling me toward them. My inner wild child who used to jump off of stair rails and onto couches was happiest when she was outside and connected to the elements of the earth—my never-ending playground!

One of my cousins and I thought it would be a good idea to go "amateur" rafting on the river using an air mattress and no life vests. After all, we had been successful with similar attempts in the past, *and* we had gone professional rafting before (one time), so we were practically experts by then. In our excitement for adventure, we forgot all of the risk that came with being in a river with high water levels. We also forgot about the 10-person team it had taken to navigate the waters successfully when we had gone professional rafting. Thinking back now, these points make the story even more embarrassing to tell!

After some successful smooth rides on the water from one stretch of the river to the other (about 50 feet or so), my cousin and I decided that we were going to take the "rafts" further down where we could see the white water. We had continued past the point of no return, when the water started to bounce us around on the air mattress. Moving further down the rapids meant that we were going a lot faster, and for a second we looked at each other, realizing that we had no control of ourselves or the makeshift raft we had been so confident about just seconds prior. As we hit some large rocks and dipped into a pebbly riverbed (one that would prove to be unforgiving), forward momentum ended up driving us into a section of the river that was full of collapsed trees and branches.

"Oh, shit! What have we done?" I yelled.

Just then, tall tree branches appeared out of nowhere from behind the white bubbles. The branches were sharp and pointed toward the air mattress the way a soldier would hold a bayonet up to his enemies. *Pop* went the air mattress...I mean "raft." We tumbled into the river, terrified for our lives.

I started swimming through rough rapids, trying to get into a position where my feet were in front of me (that is what we had been taught to do by the rafting instructor in case we fell in the river). However, Mother Nature was not cooperating and because the water was so high, I could barely get my head up before the rapids took me back down, almost to the riverbed itself. As if catching air wasn't already enough of a challenge, my feet became stuck between two large tree branches that were covered with rocks

As the force of the water was pushing me down, the two tree branches made a cross across my left foot, keeping the top of my head just below the waterline. I remember twisting to the side and turning my head up to look up at the sky that looked green from beneath the water. *So is this how I die?* I wondered. *God, please...no! What about the kids? Who is going to take care of them and love them as much as I do? And what about my hopes and dreams that I will never get to fulfill? Oh my god, how are the local news stations going to portray my death as a result of this act of stupidity? How embarrassing!*

No one could see me or know that I was in trouble, so I knew I had to help myself. Determined to escape this horrible way of dying, I started pushing on the tree branches with my hands and right foot. Now, these weren't normal river currents, because the water levels that year were high, it felt like I was being pushed down by a bunch of bricks. The pressure of the currents made it difficult to get into a position where I could free my leg, and I was running out of time and oxygen.

Pushing with all the strength I had in my body, I somehow managed to move the tree branch just enough to loosen my foot. Thankfully, that was enough for the force of the water pressure to knock me out of my bondage. Like a tumbleweed in water, I rotated just below the waterline a few times before I was able to come up for air. *Finally! I could breathe again!* Remembering the advice of our river raft guide from the past, I got into the foot-front position and waited for the river currents to slow down. Once they did, I quickly swam to shore as if my life depended on it.

My aunt's husband saw me struggling and helped me out of the water. I had been beaten up by the rocks in the water, and my ankle was swollen where it had been caught between the branches and the rocks. My cousin had made it out too, although her shirt was ripped to the point of almost completely exposing her. *So much for modesty!*

I stood there in awe of what had just happened. "Happy Birthday, Niggin," I whispered to myself. "You get to live this year!" Don't get me wrong, I love to frequent rivers that are tucked away in the mountains and walk across their shallow waters on hot summer days, but instead of tempting fate or pretending like I know what I am doing, now I choose to sit closer to the shore and dip my feet in. That day, I saw a view of the green sky from under the water that I will never forget. Mother Nature is beautiful and gives us so many gifts; however, I now recognize that she *is not* to be toyed with...unless you are ready to end your life.

I am also happy to report that no amateur rafting has taken place in my life since then. These games with death were a clear sign for me to pay attention. Life is still an adventure, but I can do great things and grow as a person without putting my life at risk. Making better choices, such as sticking to a professional white-water rafting company to take you on the river, or not buying a motorcycle to run away from your problems, are good examples for all of us to follow! Being authentic does not mean you aren't responsible for the choices you make in your life.

Sometimes it's difficult to appreciate all the blessings you have in your life when you don't pay attention to what is in front of you. I had blocked out the voices of gratitude and started to long for things that were not authentic to who I was. In this state of self-deception, I overlooked gifts such as time, love, and relationships with the people around me. Lucky for me, it only took a few difficult lessons for me to learn that I didn't have to risk my life to feel alive.

29

Walking Up the Downward Spiral

As I started to put the puzzle pieces of my life back together, I made a conscious choice to clean up my act and become more self-aware. The partying, drinking, and pill-popping had to stop if I was going to start dealing with my problems instead of avoiding them. That also meant that I had to cut ties with many of my "American" friends. Some became angry at my dismissal and others could have cared less, but it was an important step for me to be able to focus all of my energy on stabilizing my soul and understanding the impact of my unsteady emotional state. Like a ball of tangled yarn, the unravelling had to happen one breath at a time, one hour at a time, and one day at a time. I started revisiting the little Afghan-American girl who was living in the basement of my heart.

The dependence I had developed on nicotine, alcohol, and a variety of other controlled substances took time to overcome, but when I re-immersed myself into the role of a mother, the addictions faded more quickly than I had expected. Although it was painful, I welcomed the voices of reason back on the journey of my life again. This time it was me in the driver's seat, not the different identities I had developed over the years. On my way home from work one afternoon, I stopped by my hair stylist. "Pari, can you dye my hair back to my natural black color please?" The Persian-American woman gave me a sweet joyful look I will never forget.

"Of course Niggin jan!" She used the word *jan*—a term of endearment translated to mean *dear*. I was happy someone was calling me Niggin dear once again. Within a few months the light toned makeup and hyperpigmented eye shadows were stored in my makeup stash under the sink. I didn't seem to need them much anymore.

Conversations between me and God once again began to sound like prayers from a position of trust and gratitude instead of my never-ending whining. I could finally stop throwing my temper tantrum because I had learned to listen to what my teenage self had to say without harshly judging her. When that happened, I did not have anything to rebel against anymore. Slowly, a blanket of acceptance covered my body, protecting me from self-blame, guilt, and fear.

Don't misunderstand…the voices in my head were present then and they will always be exist, but I decided to stop being so hard on myself for the choices and mistakes I made in the past. Destiny placed me with my family, and I realized that I didn't need to be anyone else but myself to be happy and successful. Any lingering thoughts and questions about the road of life turned into quiet meditations, and my perspective changed. Spending time in deep thought and prayer changed my outlook, as it had done before in my younger years. There was finally peace and calm, and I moved from being on the outside of the storm and closer to the eye of the storm.

Stepping into Womanhood

When I filed for divorce and took full custody of the children, Shabir didn't show up in court to challenge me. I do not doubt the process was painful for him, but his passivity and unwillingness to deal with our relationship problems made me happy and angry all at once. I sat in the cold courtroom with other divided couples who were arguing about alimony and child support, and I let out a sarcastic laugh because we didn't have any money to fight over. My most precious valuables in this world were my three children.

I reflected on how we had spent years trying to make it work "for the kids" and ended up doing more harm than good. In my search to discover who I was, independent from a broken marriage, I had overlooked what my children needed most: a stable mother who would fight for them and listen to their needs. My mission was set, and I took control of the forward momentum, choosing to become 100 percent responsible for my children that day forward.

When the judge called my case number, I approached the bench to defend my civil request for legal independence alone; a party of one. There were no lawyers or irate in-laws in sight when I stood in front of the judge to explain what "irreconcilable differences" meant to me. "Your honor, my husband and I have spent 10 years trying to make our relationship work, but a combination of his passivity and mental health problems, and my need for stability and protection of my children is what brings me here today." I knew that no explanation could ever satisfy a stranger, let alone my extended family, so I only shared the bare minimum.

I left the courthouse wearing a DAF (Divorced Afghan Female) badge, feeling like Hester Prynne in *The Scarlet Letter*. The badge came with the territory, so I walked out accepting that it was now a part of what it meant for me to let go of the "good girl" persona that had once controlled my life for so long. I could feel the pendulum of my life swinging back to the middle. Life on either side of the extreme was gone.

Alternative Career

As part of my transformation, I chose to leave my well-paying corporate job to work for a small nonprofit organization. The thought of giving back to my community gave me a sense of joy, and though the pay cut was painful, the job allowed me to be available to my kids after school. Time was the most precious commodity, and I dedicated all of my energy to being truly present and supporting the development of my children.

My career change didn't feel like a successful move in the beginning. One week prior to my first day on the job, I had been defending a cutthroat health insurance company to a panel of federal agents who did not mince words. When I walked into my new workplace, I was met by my smiling boss who asked me to make thank you baskets for our donors.

"Sure!" I replied. I eagerly packed the branded swag into the basket and tied it with a pretty red and blue bow.

"Thanks, Shahira! Can you take this stack of cards and start writing 'Thank you' and 'Happy birthday' on them?"

"Umm, sure," I replied. *Oh shit*, I thought to myself. *Did I just make the worst mistake of my life? I can't write my next school business paper on thank you cards!* We were moving at the pace of government, and I had to slow down just enough to pay attention to the struggles of the human plight. It was time for me to learn what the word *humble* really meant.

Over time, I came to work with judges, lawyers, social workers, and other professionals from all walks of life. I researched hundreds of case studies that proved that no matter how "messed up" or dysfunctional families seemed to be, children had a better sense of identity as adults when they stayed at home instead of going into foster care. As long as the children were free from physical abuse and neglect, sometimes the imperfect parents were the only ones that could help the children be successful.

As an advocate coordinator, I managed the volunteers who were responsible for helping the overburdened caseworkers and children's lawyers. I learned about relationships and how to communicate your value proposition. The nonprofit agency I was working with had been community and grant funded. Being an advocate coordinator allowed me to work mainly with affluent White Americans who had a comfortable life and wanted to do their part to help make the world just a little bit better. Every person I met had a story to tell, and I treasured the conversations like golden nuggets and placed them in my tool bag of life.

In a one-room office, housed inside space that had been donated by a courthouse, my coworkers and I talked about the abuse children in our own backyards were suffering from. We cried together when little kids were taken from their homes and bawled real tears of sorrow if kids were sexually abused. My coworkers became my group therapy, and also friends for life.

I taught the diversity and inclusion component of advocate trainings, and it was the most fun I'd had in my career. I would get up in front of a class of 20 to 40 people, and we would have a conversation about race and prejudice. Making people uncomfortable with the truth was becoming my specialty, and the training gave me a platform to share about the fact that all of us have prejudices and imperfections. I would ask where the origin of each person's name came from, and it would give me a glimpse into the rich heritage that was present in all of us.

It was also an eye-opening experience for many people to see *a huge* PowerPoint slide display the amount of minority children versus White children within the social services system. We talked about the disparate number of Black and Hispanic children who had been removed from their homes and placed in foster homes. It gave us pause to ask, "Why is this happening?"

Training a room of older White men and women taught me more about myself than anything else. We were all prejudiced in one way or another, but if you were self-aware of those preconceived disparities and put them aside when it mattered, you could still help those who needed it. Like my mother, I was a teacher at my core, and my students were always engaged. I really enjoyed working with adults who genuinely wanted to learn about things that were important in the world. People would tell me they loved working with me and learning with me because I was a calming presence, and practice active listening. Never good at receiving praise, I typically brushed their compliments aside. I felt like I was getting entirely too much credit.

My own parenting skills were sharpening, although some would argue that I was becoming over-protective. At the age of 10, my son would come along with me to see presentations on what drugs do to the human body. I urged my young daughters, aged eight and six at the time, to call their private parts their "vaginas" and "breasts." That way, should a perpetrator ever dare touch them, they would be able to say those words clearly to me or the authorities. My protective mommy instincts were on overdrive, but I embraced it. Things were starting to change, and I was finding my balance. I no longer wanted to escape from my life, and I actually started to love the crazy person I was.

I stayed close to my roots by speaking to God more often through formal prayer. As part of my healing process, I went back to all of my foundational knowledge about religion. Instead of categorizing everything in life as *right* or *wrong* and *good* or *bad*, I focused more on the journey and the meaning of it all. I realized that going back to the key values and initial philosophical teachings I had once adhered to would give me a good foundation to rebuild my identity as a Muslim and to simply be a good person again. My American identity taught me tenacity and determination, and I wanted to create a new definition for being a Muslim-American woman in America. I knew it would take hard work and patience, especially on days when I didn't feel like facing the world as it was, but I had faith that things would work out because I had taken the action that was necessary to make it happen.

The inner playful child inside of me was coming out to play again, and no one was going to stop her from finding adventures in every aspect of life.

30

Solace on the Slopes

I became a lot like my father, taking my kids for adventures in the mountains on the weekends. We took up snowboarding and skiing, and while it was expensive on a nonprofit salary, we really enjoyed spending the time together. I bought us all used gear, and the kids would practice on the bunny slopes. Once in a while, when I had extra money, I would spend it on skiing or snowboarding lessons so that my kids could learn how to do it the right way. Lucky for my tiny savings account, they picked it up quickly and became better than me within a few lessons.

The nearest slopes were two hours away from our home, so we spent a lot of time in the car talking to each other. I learned more about what my kids liked and what they didn't like. Though they each revealed their unique personalities, I could see my mom's influence in their speech and behavior. Ironically, I became the nerdy parent that insisted we sing a song in the car together (cue

Billy Joel, or in my case, Johnny Cash) or talk about our emotions.
I was curious to understand how they perceived me as a mother
and how they felt about their absent father. It was important to me
that the children felt loved as much as they deserved to be loved.

While the kids spent all day taking lessons, my brother and
I would take the ski lifts to the highest point of the mountain and
just sit on top of the world and gaze upon life happening below. If
it was daytime, we would stare at the horizon of endless snow-covered
mountains with perfectly manicured pine trees poking out
from the slopes. When we went skiing at night, there was usually
a pink hue that would come from all the lights reflecting off the
white clouds and ground below. There was so much peace to be
found in the mountains, and I took time to reflect and appreciate
where I was in my life. While I don't go snowboarding as often
these days, heading to the mountains gives me as much peace now
as it did back then.

Money isn't everything, but pay your bills on time!

During my first year at the nonprofit, I learned a very core life
lesson: money isn't everything. Since I was earning a lot less than
I was used to, I had to learn to budget and make the most out of
my very small paycheck. Ironically, my credit had been at its worst
while I was making more money, because I was young and distracted
by everything that was happening around me. The divorce had
also put me in a financially vulnerable situation, and paying bills
became solely my responsibility. I knew that it was important for
me to build my credit if I wanted to have the opportunity to buy
my own house someday or if I wanted a nicer car for my family.

While in the corporate world, I didn't care anything about
my credit or financial future. A 401(k) was simply a type of savings
account, and retirement was so far away that I never thought about

it. When I had money, I was spending it left and right on clothes, motorcycles, makeup, and fancy dinners. I wasn't thinking about savings or putting money aside for emergencies.

Debt collectors started calling and demanding their money or threatening to defile my credit. It was painful answering the calls and negotiating terms, but I knew that just like all of my other problems, I had to deal with my finances in order to move forward. I took it one day at a time and decided to tackle what I could. When I would receive a tax refund, I would use the money to pay back my debts because I wanted to live a life of integrity and financial freedom someday. While I lived with my mom, I made sure I was being a good partner by contributing toward rent and other bills. When I had some money left over, I would put it aside to pay off the credit card debt that had accumulated during my years of frivolity. I had learned to repair my credit on a small budget. Imagine that!

I often think about the concept of abundance and wonder why it revealed itself to me during a time when I was making the least amount of money. My outlook on financial freedom changed over time, and I started spending my money on the right things. I valued things that were important, like time with my children and family, and worked on a plan that brought me to a better place; not overnight, but over time. Money isn't everything, and I am a living, breathing example of this.

Remember this lesson well. If you want to change your financial situation, and if you have the drive to learn and grow, *you can* change your course for the better. You just need to give yourself a chance to start somewhere, and then take little steps toward short-term goals. Before you know it, those big mountains of debt will appear as small as mole hills. The desire, drive, and determination to make it work are half the battle.

Propelling Forward

While I was happy at the nonprofit, I wanted to grow my career and diversify my experiences as a professional. The nonprofit world had forced me to slow down to the rate of government, which was great for my life at the time, but not for my career aspirations. I was craving the fast-paced business world and found myself reading the *Wall Street Journal* and *The New York Times* to feed my curiosity. Realizing that I would have to stay in the nonprofit world a lot longer if I wanted to move into a leadership position, I started considering other options. Aside from that, the nonprofit world would require living on a minimal income, and while Shabir was helping every now and then, it was inconsistent, and the kids' needs were growing.

My job seemed to be costing me opportunities for growth, and I wanted to do more. Not in a selfish way, but I knew that my talents were being under used, and if I wanted long-term financial stability, I would need to find a better job. After a few years of playing it safe while I rebuilt my foundation of inner peace, I decided to pursue my master's degree in business and move my career back into the corporate world. I was ready to join the business conversation again and place my energy and focus on helping others grow.

No Men, Please

I had a master plan. I was going to travel the world with my three children and raise them on the road without a partner. My gypsy soul was looking for adventure again, so I looked for jobs that would take me around the world. I knew I had the skills to meet any business goal I set my mind to, and I was confident that I knew how it was going to turn out. While it wasn't a practical plan, I had started dreaming of an adventurous life again, and the spark of excitement I once had as a child was returning. My curiosity was at its peak, and I had a vision boiling in my blood. The solace provided by those Rocky Mountains allowed me space to breathe and start living my life on a path that I would never regret.

My marriage ending in shambles had left me a bit bitter in the relationship department. The American men I had met in previous years—whether at school, work, or through friends— were on a different level of thinking. One dinner date or a few phone calls was all it took to dismiss the idea of a serious relationship. Men I knew appeared to be after the very material things in life, and I just couldn't relate. After sharing a few sentences about my life, the dating prospect would usually say, "Three kids, you say? Oh, look at the time! I have to meet my friend in an hour. It was nice to meet you." I would laugh as they would walk away and I'd pat myself on the back for managing to scare off each new guy quicker than the last.

I kept thinking to myself, *How can anyone ever relate to me?* Slowly but surely, my faith in the opposite gender began to fade. Truth be told, I was underdeveloped and immature in the relationship department myself. The only relationship I had really known had turned into a horror story, and I wasn't ready to expose myself or my children to that again. I promised myself that I would not bring anyone into our lives who didn't love us all completely. It was my way of keeping my heart intact and my children safe from all the crazy in the world.

Unexpected Blessings of Friendship

One day on the slopes, while snowboarding with my brother, I received a message from a person who I had known many moons before. I certainly had not expected to hear from him, but he had taken the time to write me! The only thing that was missing was the envelope and postage stamp. "I always wondered what happened to you, and I am glad to see that you and your family look so happy in your pictures," his message read, along with belated condolences for my father's death.

As I read the message, a flashback of a distant memory hit me. I was a 14-year-old girl at my cousin's house for her engagement party. My oldest cousin was about to marry a complete stranger, and this was the first time we were going to meet his family. While she was getting ready to wear her beautiful pink gown upstairs, I was sent down to help my mom serve tea to the groom's family and guests. As I walked down the steps, I looked out at the living room filled with the unfamiliar faces of other Afghan families I didn't recognize.

One particular boy caught my eye. He was wearing an electric blue suit. I had never seen him or that shade of blue before that moment and was intrigued by how he stood out. As I moved my eyes from his suit to his face, I found the attractive, tan, and skinny 16-year-old was looking back at me as well. As the trail of stairs ended, I took my eyes off of him and moved into the kitchen to help my mom.

As a 14-year-old Afghan daughter, my job was clear. I served tea, fruit, and dessert to all the guests. When passing out cups of tea, you always start with the oldest person in the room and move to the youngest. Since there were 50 people in the room that night, I had some time before I would offer him his cup. As I moved from the oldest to the youngest, my grip on the serving tray became shaky. I was totally crushing, and hoped he didn't notice when my flushed, red face approached his crooked smiling face. Quickly, I ran back to the kitchen and made myself busy with other guest-related duties. *Who is that guy?* I wondered.

His name was Qais, but he went by Q. He was the groom's brother. Because of our cultural limitations, we never communicated beyond "Hi" and "Goodbye."

"Ready to go?" asked my brother, tapping my shoulder and bringing me back to present day.

I read and reread the message, reminiscing about the old memories from years ago. I was pondering why Q had reached out, and I wasn't even sure if I was going to respond. What was I going to say to him? I kept thinking I should write him back and say, "Don't congratulate me on my marriage. I'm a DAF!"

I had just recovered from being a mess, and I wasn't ready to tell anyone about my past. The thought of vulnerability scared me until I remembered how warm I had once felt around him. I took my time responding to him and didn't disclose any details about what had occurred in my life. After a few messages, he gathered that my situation was complicated, and we agreed to stay connected as friends.

To my surprise, Q was unlike any other man I knew, let alone other Afghan men. He lived in Chicago close to his sister and nephews and spoke about them with such love and endearment. Not only was he intelligent, but he was also articulate, and he had no problem expressing confidence in his identity as an Afghan-American. I was intrigued.

I was always amazed when anyone spoke with such conviction, especially those who came from a diverse ethnic background, because I knew how difficult it was to live without it. Other Afghan or Middle Eastern men I knew were chauvinistic and had strict, conservative views on women and their role in society as well as the family dynamic. Q spoke so passionately about his liberal views and current events in the world, and I wondered why he never became a teacher or a professor. We sometimes spent hours into the night discussing politics, new scientific discoveries, or how American values had impacted who we are. I was amazed at how small the world was and how this person I barely knew from years ago was back in my life.

Q was a history and geography buff, so he taught me a lot about Afghan and American history. We talked about dreams that had been shattered over the years and how we both had experienced disappointment following a path that was not "Afghan" enough in our lives. Just like me, he loved his family dearly and made it a priority to create more connections to them over the years. *Imagine that*, I thought to myself. *Here is someone who grew up with a very similar history and childhood as me, yet his views are liberal and progressive.*

What is this thing called?

Within a few months of talking with Q, I started to develop deeper feelings than friendship for him. From a thousand miles away, he urged me to be strong and stick to being myself, even in moments that I felt my family was pushing me to make decisions that I didn't agree with. Whenever I placed limitations on myself, he shattered them as well as any doubts that I had about achieving my goals. Sometimes he was the only one who reminded me that I was good enough just being me and that my struggles were valid. When I would call Q for advice, he always took the time to listen before he would respond with his opinion. I didn't have to explain what it felt like to be Afghan and American, so we always skipped the small talk and conversed on the deep-seated insecurities we both had.

Q's perspective couldn't have been more different than mine, but he had Afghan-American sisters and he was well aware of the double standards that existed in our culture. He never pretended to know what I was going through as a woman and offered to discuss any topic that was considered blacklisted in the Afghan community. We had creative debates into the night and for the first time in my life, someone was bold enough to challenge me on my beliefs and identity, and I was growing as a person. To make matters more interesting, we were in a cultural transgression because we were in a long-distance relationship.

One day during a random moment I realized that I had fallen in love with Q. We were discussing a problem I was having with my son who was similar in age to Q's nephew, and it hit me like an adrenaline rush. Though our phone conversation had come to an end, I did not want to say goodbye, and asked him to stay on the phone with me for longer. Later that evening, when I was describing my emotional interruption from earlier that day, he paused and replied with, "Yeah, I think I love you too."

Is this really happening? I thought. *Had Prince Eric been living in Chicago all this time?*

Because we were Afghan, we had to date privately for a while. Living 1,000 miles apart was difficult, but I was able to stay at home with my children and I maintained the long-distance relationship by phone. When we were able to meet a few times in person we savored each trip with new adventures. In Chicago, he would take me on walking trips around the city and wonderful new restaurants. When he would come to Denver, I would take him on hikes and into the beautiful mountains for day trips. During one hike I remember losing the trail path, and he turned to me and said "That's ok babe, we will create our own path!" We gave each other a cheesy look because we both read between the lines on what was to come.

When a job opportunity arose, Q moved to Denver so that we could see what a face-to-face relationship would be like for us. Having Q come to Denver validated what we had originally expressed to each other on the phone, and the few times we saw each other. Being in each other's presence brought another level of love to our relationship, and I was excited and scared all at once. I appreciated the little things, like sitting across from him as I enjoyed dinner or staring at him while he drove hours into the mountains because I needed to be in nature that day. Feeling the touch of his hand while his fingers were wrapped around mine brought me a sense of security that I hadn't experienced before.

Q didn't ask me to justify who I was. He simply loved me for who I was: the edgy, misshapen, and imperfect Niggin. The thought of someone loving me for who I was made me rethink the idea of living life without a partner. *Master plans were made to be broken*, I thought.

Since the cultural stigma of dating is so negative in the Afghan culture and Muslim religion, we had to hide our relationship, and once again I was facing the same struggles of carrying secrets that only my close "American" friends were brought in on. I was also deeply afraid of how perfect the love I had found was. *Am I glamorizing the experience? What if this doesn't work out? Can I sweep it under the rug? What if I end up hurt again? Am I ready to enter a new relationship? What about love? Is this what it feels like? What if…what if… what if?* My mind was on blast again!

The matter of being in another relationship was further complicated by the fact that I was a mother of three young children. I made a promise to myself that I wasn't going to introduce them to Q until I was 100 percent sure he was the right person for our family. This meant that I couldn't assimilate him into my one life/ one identity rule unless he *really* understood that I had full custody and responsibility over my children.

We dated for two years before we formalized our intentions with both my mom and his family. As you can imagine, this became quite the shock for both sides, because no one we knew was in a similar situation. Q and I were blazing the way with our unconventional relationship. I knew what was running through the minds of my mom and siblings: I was a divorced single mom and wanted to marry some bachelor? Who was he? How was he related to the family again? Does he know Niggin has three kids? Is he the new "motorcycle" in her crazy life?

His family was thinking similarly: Why is he marrying a divorcée who has full custody of her three young children? Could he not find a better Afghan girl with less baggage? Those kids will soon be teenagers, and he will head for the hills! How long before he realizes he is making a mistake?

My mother was especially shocked when Q came over for the traditional "teatime" talk/marriage proposal. He was alone, representing himself and his family (another first). My mom decided to skip over the small talk and get straight to the point. "Why do you want to do this? This is not an easy relationship you are getting into, and taking on the responsibility of raising three children is a lot. You have no experience with this." Q was able to answer her questions, but my mom did test him fully that day. She was scared for me, for she envisioned the challenges ahead of us. While she gave her blessings to both of us that day, she did so cautiously.

Only after making clear who Q was to my mother and siblings and receiving their blessings did I introduce him to my children. We spent the afternoon having lunch and watched a movie together. Maryam, who usually carried her quarters, dimes, and nickels in a sandwich baggie, showed Q affection and approval by giving him her money, sandwich baggie and all.

When we all said goodbye to Q that day, we jumped into the car and I turned around and asked the kids, "So…what do you think?"

All three kids jumped up and down and said, "*Yes!* He is the one!"

While spending the afternoon with him was just a glance into our future, I knew he would be a good father to them. My love for him continued to grow and we decided to merge our lives together in a formal ceremony before God and our families.

Our marriage was taboo. Things like what was happening to me just don't happen. As an Afghan woman, you don't date and you don't get divorced and you don't go against cultural norms. I could hear the whispering from my extended family in the background, but I didn't care. The people who knew and spent time with us were happy for us. The man I was in love with had decided to join the ride that was my life, and I was ecstatic. "You do know I have three kids, right?" I would joke in times of self-doubt and insecurity.

For my husband, the struggle was just as intense. Being an Afghan male, also a 1.5 generation American, he knew that our relationship was not conventional. He was an eligible bachelor who was marrying a 30-something divorcée with three children. I mean, was he out of his mind? He was an eligible, good-looking single person. He was told many times by his family, and mine, that he was making a mistake, but he just shrugged his shoulders and said, "We will see." If there was ever an ounce of doubt or fear in either of us, we talked about it. We didn't know how the future would pan out, but we knew we deeply loved each other and that being together felt scary and right all at once.

While our relationship may seem perfect to some, I am here to admit we have our share of disagreements. Relationships, whether marriage or a friendship, are a human act, and by nature that makes them a flawed process. Authentic relationships provide us security in many ways; emotionally, intimately, and sexually, however there is no perfect path. The only validation we have about "doing it right" is by measuring mutually positive results. One key belief that opened my eyes to the complexity of human relationships is this: *The person you are with is a whole universe unto themselves.* Not a planet, a *universe!* To think that we can "sum a person up" or understand who they are within a few discussions is an unreal expectation. It takes time, patience, and a willingness to honor the experiences of a person from childhood to adulthood. Relationships (in whatever form) are a journey, not a destination to arrive at, so you better love and honor the person who is in the passenger seat of your life, even when they don't agree with you.

We took a chance on love, and I am glad we did because I have no doubt that I am married to my one and only Prince Eric. So, remember the title at the beginning of this chapter, *No Men Please?* As it turns out, I was fortunate enough to meet the right one.

Parenting the "Right Way"

"If you're not exhausted on a daily basis, you are not doing it right." —Me

Being married and in love means that we are on the same journey of being our best selves within the family dynamic. In the last few years, Q and I have welcomed two additional children into our family, Zoe and Ely. *Yes*, we are raising all five of our children together under one roof. People often ask me if I plan to give birth to more human beings. I tell them I have given my fair share to the cause of humanity, so there is not a plan for me to join the half-dozen club. From the teenagers to the babies, we have become parenting experts of sorts. Are we perfect? No. Have we slept a full restful night in the last few years? No. There were and continue to be challenging moments for all of us. Falling in love didn't make the day-to-day any easier, only more fulfilling, and sometimes more complicated. The older kids still have "daddy issues" because of their limited relationships with their father, and at times it is Q who is left to absorb the hurt and pick up the pieces of their broken hearts.

Life isn't sunshine and rainbows all the time; rather, it's stormy, thundery, and loud as we struggle to create the life we want. Our parenting styles are not the same, and sometimes we argue or engage in shouting matches because we don't see eye to eye on how to discipline the children. We set date nights in an effort to spend time with one another as a couple, and even with the best of planning, some nights are spent talking about the children and their latest woes. What is different, however, is our ability to understand and appreciate the strengths and weaknesses we have as partners in moments of vulnerability. I am an intuitive person and Q is a very calculated one, so we can be polar opposites in our personality traits. Love is the instrument that facilitates the understanding between us and for that reason we take time to know that about each other so we can be better (more aligned) parents. I have so much gratitude for Q and all the love he has given to our family. I could probably write a whole other book on parenting and relationships! We both work very hard on being there for each other, and we are committed to being better parents on a *daily* basis.

The Beauty of Chaos

My days are hectic but beautiful. The three older children, now going into their own young adulthood, require emotional support almost daily. The younger children require me to show up on their time, and test our physical stamina 24/7. Sometimes the lack of sleep and constant yelling to organize the troops shows up in our puffy under eyes and messed up hair. At any given time, I could be chasing a naked baby around the house while having a conversation with my older kids about school projects, and then I move right along to washing the dishes.

Through it all, I remember that the children I am raising are little adults. They are becoming beautiful human beings, who may also identify as Multi-Americans. I want nothing more than for my kids to have an uncompromising identity and to know that their parents will love them no matter what. If there is any unconditional love that I believe exists in this world, it is that of a mother to her child.

I often look at my children through sleep-deprived eyes, but I would not change it for the world. Some of our conversations involve gender role identities and traditional Afghan roles versus modern American roles. Sometimes we find ourselves in similar battles with our children that our parents had with us, though in our family, we define gender roles from a more biological standpoint and less of a social one.

The children see me working a traditional job outside of the home, alongside my husband. We communicate to our children that husbands and wives can make choices as individuals, but that they must respect each other enough to discuss the other person's perspective. We talk about consent and what that means in a casual setting, as well as from an intimacy standpoint. We do not restrict any traditionally taboo topics such as sex and relationships, and because of that, we have a different connection with our older children than our parents had with us.

Although I am the primary cook at home, my husband steps in and helps when I ask him to. When it's his turn, he whips up his killer quesadillas or dials up the local pizza place, and we sit down and eat together. Cooking and cleaning are helpful life skills for *all humans* to have, and that is the lesson we make clear to our children instead of the lesson I learned growing up of, "*You should learn to cook and clean because you are a girl and you need to do it for your future husband and his family.*" Sully, who is now a teenager, makes most of his own meals because self-efficacy and self-compassion are themes I preach to him daily.

The Beauty of Educating the Mind

It took me 12 years to obtain my bachelor's degree, and a few more years after that for my MBA. Through the years of difficulties and struggles, I pushed through because it was *that* important to me. Years of my mother's sound advice stuck in my head and helped me get through some long nights of typing research papers. Her words have become a motto of sorts in my life, roughly translated from Dari to mean, "Whether you do it or not, the time will pass, so just do it." While not very poetic, her words reflect her playful personality and remind me of a Rumi poem that reads:

> **"Though your heart grows weary**
> **And you tire of life-**
> **O time waster**
> **This is a journey you cannot avoid."**

When I walked down the aisle to be handed my MBA, Q and my immediate family were there to cheer me on. I was pregnant with my fourth child, Zoe. With one hand on my growing belly and the other with a degree in hand, the sky was the limit. I would raise my daughters and sons differently and create an ongoing narrative about how they did not have to be perfect humans, only genuine ones. I would teach them that the most important factor in their lives is to live with authentic purpose and inner peace.

While my MBA doesn't come from a prestigious Ivy League school, it did come with hard work and late nights of reading through business books, writing leadership essays on organizational change, gender equity in the workplace, and listening to long lectures. My effort as a nontraditional student was no less than a younger person in a traditional setting, and I was proud of my accomplishment. I dared to be different and confident in my own set of standards, and that is what brought me success. No matter what work I did, how much money I made, what car I drove, or what house I lived in, I was grateful for the opportunity to grow and have a unique perspective as a student. (Cue me jumping up and throwing my hat in the air, as I hear, "Congratulations, class of 2014!")

Defining Me

"Honor Your Heritage, But Be the Story-teller of Your Own Life"

My journey toward authenticity and self-awareness started when I kicked the idea of being a "good girl" to the curb. I realized that I was a combination of all of my experiences: the good, bad, and the ugly. I would never say that I have "arrived" because I believe in an ongoing growth mindset, but here I am, nearing my 40s and fulfilling every single goal I have set for myself.

While others in the world are defining what it means to be Afghan or Muslim, I am lucky enough to define what it means to be both Afghan-American and Muslim-American woman. The spirit of my father is still present in me, and because of his influence, I will never stop going on adventures. Because of my parents, I will never underestimate the power of love and how it transforms people to be compassionate. I appreciate and honor the position my dad and mom were in to do the best they could to raise us; however, I am also aware the journey for my family is different. As an Afghan-American and Muslim-American I *can* relate to my children in a way that my father never could to us. I do not have a traditional Afghan mindset, and I do not use guilt or fear tactics to punish my family for the decisions they make. Instead, I value autonomy and understand the importance of tolerance and independence. It is in these differences that I remain authentic to my own essence and combined value systems.

As an Afghan-American woman, I am surrounded by the grace of strong Afghan women who demonstrate resilience and perseverance in everyday actions. My mom continues to be a rock for our family and nurtures the people around her without asking for anything in return. Her strength and enduring soul provide a compass for me and my girls when we need grounding guidance. My mom and I are different people, but there is a relationship of love and authenticity where there used to be a façade of emotions and blame. I recognize that she is the force that pulled me through some difficult times. Today my mom often consults me on how she should interact with my siblings, and it is the small moments I appreciate how far we have come in our own relationship.

Finding My Voice

Now that you know the backstory, why does it matter?

Ask anyone who knows me what kind of person I am, and they will probably describe me as being bossy, stubborn, caring, resourceful, giving, sarcastic, and highly determined to make things work. I am usually the one engaging in debates, speaking my truth, and making the people around me uncomfortable. I come from a long and proud history of strong-willed women, and I always knew in my heart that someday the strength of my heritage would lead me to my authentic American identity and purpose. The tragic truth is, it took me entirely too long to know and live my truth. Not talking about our own human difficulties for fear being too American did *not* make our problems disappear, it only kept us in the Comfort Zone, for fear of what an authentic life would mean in the context of our identities. Denial can be a strong shield; however, it is not strong enough to eradicate reality.

While Afghanistan has been in the media for less than desirable reasons in the last two decades, it is a big part of who I am and why I think the way I do. There was an inner child within me trying to find her way out, and sometimes she felt ripped apart between both cultures. My story is a real-life example of why women from restricting cultures who grow up in more liberal societies, like America, encounter identity issues. The Multi-American perspective is important, but it can only be cultivated and heard when we value our experiences as a necessary part of the American story. In order to build a world that is more equitable for women, we must be willing to overcome the mindset that being an American person means we have to melt into the proverbial American pot and deny our cultural roots. The truth is that America is made up of multi-ethnic, racial, and religious people and views, and the more we can empower women to uncover the internal "tug-of-war" with their identities, the quicker and more effective we become as successful Americans who can help reach across borders and bridge gaps for our families, and for the larger global community.

I hope my story serves as inspiration for you, dear reader, to break out of your shell and live the life you've always wanted. They say ambition is the birth of dreams, so remember all the dreams you had as a child and find the courage to question the world and the possibilities it holds for you. I'm in your corner, and when you find your place, nestled securely between two different flags or markers, you are home. Embrace and value the freedom to not have to choose between them or fit within boundaries, because this is what it means to be *American*.

Now that I have told you my story, I ask you, what is yours?

Home

A poem by Asiyah Eeman

I am the second child, and eldest daughter of Afghan parents.
I am Eeman.

My origins come from Kabul, Afghanistan; the land of conflict and beauty; the land where dancing is a never-ending tradition; where the mountains will take your breath away with a single glance.

But with the beauty comes conflict.
Like the war that tore my family away from that beauty of that land.
As the war tore us away, we were stitched into a different place.

Like a wind carrying the leaves and seeds of a tree far far away.
Where the seeds depart from their mother and settle in a place that a new tree would make most impact.
Here we are, in the *land of the free, and the home of the brave* which we call **Home.**
America, she wraps us in her freedom and beauty, and she keeps us safe in her arms.

Even at Home, every so often, I feel the waters of Afghan rivers flowing through me like it is a part of who I am.

Even at Home, every so often, I feel my ancestors calling me. The elders.
They whisper to me about the culture that lies beneath the different layers of myself.

I long for the gatherings that are filled with laughter.
The joy and conversations that go late into night.
The taste and smell of sharing homemade Kabuli Palau.

But here is Home.
At Home, in the *land of the free* I get to be who I want!
I pursue education.
I express my emotions without breaking the laws of mankind.
I value becoming a woman who can change a community without being judged for my gender.

My blood will always crave the astonishing culture of Afghanistan, a place full of laughter and joy.

But here, here, here is where I belong.

About the Author

Shahira Niggin Qudrat is a cross-cultural leadership guide and consultant for Multi-American women who desire to excel in corporate leadership while defusing cultural blocks and self-limiting beliefs and juggling dual identities. She provides corporate consulting, workshops, and one-on-one mentorship that demystifies cultural nuances within the workplace and helps women with dual identities grow and excel.

Shahira is also the founder of Multi-American Moxie, an organization that helps develop first- & second-generation American women who desire to live in their zone of authenticity. As a thought leader, motivational speaker, and role model for women who struggle to exist within dual cultures, Shahira teaches them to navigate life within dual cultures and embrace their roots along with their American identity.

Active in community service, Shahira spends time aiding refugee families in their transition to American life. With an MBA under her belt, she also serves as a business leader who merges passion with purpose. With over 15 years in private and non-profit business sectors, her own core strengths include organizational change management, high functioning team development, business strategy planning, and project management. Shahira is also passionate about her roles as a mother, wife, sister, and daughter. She and her husband reside in Denver, Colorado, where they are raising their five beautiful children.

For tools, resources, discussion guides and more, visit http://www.AuthenticityinAmerica.com/resources.

About the Artist

Roya Saberzada is an artist and women's rights activist from Mazar-e-Sharif, a city in the northern part of Afghanistan. Roya discovered her own authentic purpose at the age of 15, when she began to draw and paint her interpretation of struggles facing the women in her society. Roya's compelling art has been featured in several exhibitions in Afghanistan and Europe, opening the public's eyes to the global struggles of violence against women.

Roya is a political science major at her university and a volunteer member of FWW (Free Women Writers). She is highly active in civil society events at her school and in her community. When Roya is not busy changing the world one piece of art at a time, she enjoys spending time with her family and traveling the world.

Acknowledgments

In true Muslim fashion, I start all things with Bismilahi Rahmani Rahim. (In the Name of God, Most Merciful, Most Kind.) I am grateful and privileged beyond measure. Writing a book and reliving personal history is no small feat. It requires no less than a village of people to bring a book to life, and I am thankful to those who have become a part of my journey as a result of this project.

First and foremost, a great measure of gratitude is due to my wonderful family who has supported me through this process. A special thank you to my husband Qais; my best friend who made me laugh, wiped my tears, held me tight, and cheered me on during some difficult moments. Thank you to my beautiful children who kept me strong and focused on the end goal. They took care of each other when Mom was busy writing her book, and I am honored to be the mother of some of the most wonderful human beings I know. And to my mom, Nooria, thank you. She is the link to my history, an honorable woman, and an upstanding human being. I strive to be more like her every day. To my siblings, thank you for your support. Destiny gave us an emotional bond that can never be replaced, and I am thankful for the lifelong friendship I have with each of you. To my uncles, aunts, and cousins who are always cheering me on, thank you! Each of you has a place in my heart and I am forever grateful you are a part of my story.

To the team of experts, mentors, and editors who guided me along the way, thank you! A special thank you to Dr. Nahid Aziz, Kate Rouze, Desiree Fitzpatrick, Olivia Omega Wallace, and Bob Tomes for paving the way for my story and guiding me to dive deeper into the message. I could not have done this without you. Thank you to Pete Zahurak for producing the cover art better than what I imagined it to be. To my many friends and colleagues who turned into informal counselors in this process, thank you! To my publisher, thank you for your patience and confidence in my story. And last but not least, thank you to Roya Saberzada, the remarkable artist of the images within the pages of this book. Roya is a young Afghan woman who embodies the true spirit of the new generation of women in Afghanistan. May she and other activists like her engaged in the fight for humanity be successful in the soul-binding endeavor for peace and compassion.